DO WE LIVE, OR JUST EXIST?

REFLECTIONS FROM A LIFE THAT BECAME MERE SURVIVAL

TITUS NAZARENE KUJUR

To Madeline,

Your laughter is the melody of sunshine, your energy a whirlwind of joy. You remind me that life is meant to be lived freely, without hesitation—dancing through moments, dreaming without limits, and embracing every adventure with wide-eyed wonder.

May you always hold on to your boundless spirit, your endless curiosity, and your beautiful way of turning the ordinary into magic. This book is for you, my little whirlwind of light.

Contents

Contents

Contents

Contents

Contents

Contents

Foreword

Life moves swiftly, often pulling us along without pause, leaving us to wonder—are we truly living, or merely existing? In the rush of responsibilities and ambitions, we sometimes forget to stop, to breathe, to notice the beauty around us. Do We Live, or Just Exist? is a collection of poetry that dares to ask this question, offering reflections on the dreams we chase, the moments we overlook, and the quiet wisdom hidden in everyday life.

These poems speak to the heart of human experience—of longing, wonder, resilience, and the need to slow down and truly feel. They remind us that living is not just about movement, but about presence. Whether through the wonders of nature, the depths of imagination, or the simple joys of childhood, this book invites you to step away from the noise and rediscover what it means to truly be alive.

As you turn these pages, may you find yourself pausing, reflecting, and seeing the world with new eyes. And perhaps, by the end, you will have your own answer to the question—Do we live, or do we just exist?

Preface

In the rush of life, we chase dreams like fireflies, hoping to grasp their glow before they fade into the distance. We measure time in accomplishments, moments in milestones, and existence in the echoes of what we leave behind. But somewhere between chasing and reaching, between striving and surviving, we often forget to pause. To breathe. To truly see.

Do We Live, or Just Exist? is not just a question—it is a reflection of the life we lead. It is a call to step beyond routine, to awaken from the trance of mere existence, and to embrace the beauty hidden in the ordinary. This collection of poems is born from that awakening—the realization that life is not just about running toward distant horizons but also about cherishing the path beneath our feet.

I have written these verses as a mirror to the world I see, the emotions I feel, and the moments that often go unnoticed. These poems speak of dreams pursued, of time slipping away, of the longing to capture fleeting beauty, and of the silent wisdom whispered by the universe to those who choose to listen.

May these words remind you that life is more than a race—it is a journey meant to be felt, not just travelled. That in the stillness of a sunrise, in the laughter of a stranger, in the rhythm of the rain, and in the quiet ache of longing, we find traces of something greater than existence—we find the essence of truly living.

So, take a breath. Look around. And ask yourself—Do you live, or do you just exist?

Acknowledgements

No book is born in isolation, and this one is no exception. It has been shaped not only by my own experiences but also by the inspiration and encouragement of those around me. Among them, two individuals stand out—**Soham Kar and Khushi Saha**—whose talent, passion, and creativity have deeply influenced my journey as a writer.

Soham Kar is a rare blend of intellect and artistry. A brilliant student with an insatiable curiosity for knowledge, he excels in academics while also possessing the soul of a poet. His words carry wisdom beyond his years, and his ability to articulate thoughts—both in writing and speech—is nothing short of remarkable. Beyond poetry, he finds expression in music, skilfully playing the guitar, weaving melodies that echo the emotions of his verses. His talent as an orator, his depth of thought, and his relentless pursuit of excellence continue to inspire me.

Khushi Saha, on the other hand, brings colour and life to the world through her art. A gifted painter, she has earned well-deserved recognition, winning numerous prizes for her breathtaking creations. Yet, her artistry is not confined to the canvas alone—her poetry, much like her paintings, captures emotions with delicate precision, painting vivid images with words. A brilliant student with an unwavering dedication to her craft, she embodies the beauty of creativity in its purest form.

Both Soham and Khushi remind me that true talent knows no boundaries—that art, poetry, and intellect can exist in harmony, shaping perspectives and touching hearts. Their passion has been a guiding force, encouraging me to bring this collection to life.

To everyone who has walked with me on this creative journey, offering support, encouragement, and belief in the power of words—thank you. This book is for all who seek inspiration, for those who embrace both the light and the shadow, and for those who find beauty in the poetry of life.

With heartfelt gratitude,

Titus Nazarene Kujur

1. The Veil of Courage

The king with crown upon his brow,
Claims bravery in every vow.
He speaks of courage, bold and grand,
But shields of steel are in his hand.
For what is strength without a sword,
What is a monarch without the horde?
Even the mightiest heart shall know,
The fear that whispers soft and low.
For courage isn't just the fight,
It's facing shadows in the night.
A warrior's strength, a king's command,
Are fragile things in shifting sand.
He calls for armies to protect,
To guard his throne and to deflect
The storms that rage, the winds that howl,
The dangers lurking on the prowl.
And yet within his guarded heart,
A fear, a doubt, may still take part.
A man may rise and boldly stand,
But who protects when he is unmanned?
No crown, no title, no great might,
Can shield the soul from deepest fright.
For even kings, in their repose,
Are touched by fear that softly grows.

The sword, the shield, the soldier's might,
Cannot erase the darkest night.
The storm may come, the rain may fall,
And even kings may feel so small.
There is no shame in fearing deep,
For even the bravest hearts may weep.
The strength of man is not in pride,
Or in the steel he keeps inside.
It's in his courage to confess,
That even giants may feel less.
To rise, to face the truth unbowed,
Though sheltered 'neath a thundercloud.
For courage lies not in the fight,
But in the choice to face the night.
The king may reign, the monarch rule,
But in their hearts, they're still the fool,
If they refuse to see the fear,
That makes us human, makes us dear.
There's power in the simple truth,
That all may tremble, all may soothe.
No shame in saying "I am small,"
For in that truth, we rise, we call.
For courage is not the absence of dread,
But the strength to move where angels tread.
So wear your armour, raise your shield,
But never let your truth be sealed.
A mighty king, a fearless knight,
Are those who face the endless fight.
And in their hearts, they know the cost—

That courage comes when fear is lost.
Not in the sword, nor in the crown,
Not in the might to hold it down,
But in the humble, tender plea,
To see the truth that sets you free.
For even kings, in their repose,
Are touched by fear that softly grows.
And when they fall, or when they rise,
They stand as human, with open eyes.
The greatest strength that kings may claim,
Is knowing fear and still the same.
For in that truth, they boldly stand,
With fragile hearts, and trembling hand.

2. The Little Match Girl

Upon the streets of London's night,
In bitter cold, devoid of light,
A little girl, with heart so pure,
Set forth to sell her wares obscure.
Her hands were numb, her face so pale,
She cried her wares, a quiet wail.
"Matches for sale, to light your way,"
But no one listened, none would pay.
With hollow eyes, she walked alone,
A child of hunger, cold as stone.
The bustling crowd, so full of cheer,
Unnoticed passed the girl in fear.
Their hearts were set on joy and song,
Preparing for the night so long.
To welcome Christ, the King, the Lord,
Yet overlooked the soul ignored.
She asked for warmth, she asked for food,
But none would spare a thought or mood.
They saw her not, a street-bound face,
Only a nuisance in their place.
They hurried past, with heartless stride,
In festive cheer, they did collide.
But she, so small, so cold, alone,
Continued on, with heavy tone.

Her matchsticks flickered in the breeze,
Her eyes were clouded, desperate pleas.
The Christmas bells rang far and wide,
But she, alone, had none beside.
Her stomach hollow, her spirit frail,
She whispered prayers, a silent wail.
"Let someone see, let someone care,
Before the cold takes me somewhere."
But no one stopped, no one did pause,
As Christmas cheer gave no applause.
Her tiny hands, so pale and thin,
Clutched onto hope with trembling skin.
The streets were filled with laughter bright,
Yet she, a child, was lost to night.
Her body frail, her spirit weak,
But still she cried, so brave, so meek.
Until, at last, she felt her knees,
And fell amidst the winter's freeze.
Her little voice, so faint and small,
Cried out for warmth, but none would call.
The snow around her cold and deep,
The silence wrapped her as she wept.
Her heart was heavy, filled with pain,
Yet through the sorrow, she remained.
Then came the dogs, so wild, so free,
A pack that roamed with loyalty.
They huddled close, with gentle care,
To warm her up, to ease despair.
A steak of meat, so soft and bright,

One dog brought forth to end her plight.
A mouse, so small, so quick, so light,
Brought bread to ease her frozen night.
Yet she, with heart so full of grace,
Refused to eat, to save her place.
She fed them first, with love and care,
Her hunger gone, her heart laid bare.
For she knew love is not for gain,
It's given freely through the pain.
She held them close, no words to say,
But in her heart, she found her way.
And in that warmth, she drifted deep,
To sleep, to dream, to peaceful keep.
Her smile, so faint, a light so pure,
Her spirit free, her heart secure.
She thanked them all, with silent song,
And in their warmth, she felt so strong.
The dogs, the mice, the kindness shown,
In them, her love had fully grown.
But when the morning sun did rise,
And church bells rang through open skies,
The people passed, as they did before,
Yet saw the child, who walked no more.
Upon the street, amidst the snow,
A little girl, so still, so low.
Her smile remained, though she had died,
A peaceful joy, where pain had lied.
They knelt beside her, hearts filled with grief,
But none could answer her silent plea.

Her face was calm, no trace of fear,
Her spirit free, her heart sincere.
Yet in that smile, a message lay,
Of love and kindness every day.
For even in the darkest night,
She found her peace, her shining light.
The world may pass and not be seen,
The pain, the hunger, in between.
But kindness, love, is always near,
For those who open hearts to hear.
The little match girl, in her strife,
Showed us the beauty of a life.
Not in the wealth, nor in the song,
But in the love that carries on.
Her gift was small, yet full of grace,
She gave her warmth, she found her place.
In all the chaos, in all the noise,
She found her peace, her heart's true voice.
She taught us all, through bitter cold,
That love is given, not bought or sold.
And in the end, when all is done,
It's love that lights the darkest sun.
So let us learn from her pure soul,
To feed the hungry, make them whole.
To see the ones who cry in vain,
And feel the sorrow, feel the pain.
For in their eyes, we find our truth,
That love is not the pride of youth.
It's not the wealth, the fame, the name,

But the kindness that remains the same.
So may we walk with open eyes,
And see beyond the world's disguise.
For in each soul, a light does burn,
And in each heart, there's room to learn.
The little match girl, so cold, so kind,
Leaves us a lesson to remind.
That in the coldest, darkest night,
It's love that keeps our hearts alight.

3. The Crownless King

O mighty castle, so lone, so stark,
A beacon still, through the endless dark.
No beasts nor men dare cross your keep,
Where memories of kings forever sleep.
The land you guard lies desolate, bare,
Yet still, you linger, forever aware.
The prey you shield is not of flesh,
But time itself, in its endless mesh.
You rise, a sentinel bound by stone,
A monument to what was once known.
Your roar is silent, yet loud it rings,
A hymn to forgotten queens and kings.
Through storms and stars, through dusk and dawn,
You remain, though your lords are gone.
No mortal reign can your spirit confine,
A fortress eternal, the years define.
And as I gaze, the world stands still,
Your presence commands my trembling will.
A crownless king, yet a king you are,
A lonely star, no matter how far.
The sun sets low, the shadows blend,
Your tale, O castle, will never end.
In barren lands, where few would tread,
You rise as a sovereign of the dead.
The winds may strip, the rains erode,
Yet you remain, a timeless ode.
A testament to what stands tall,
When kingdoms crumble and empires fall.

O Crownless King, with silent grace,
Your majesty no age can displace.
Forever you'll stand, a mark of time,
A fortress eternal, a song sublime.

4. Through You, I See the World

You are my eyes; through you, I see,
A vast, bright world of endless beauty.
With your wings, I could soar so high,
Touching the clouds, reaching the sky.
You move with grace, unbound, unchained,
Unaware of battles lost or gained.
You don't know when to fight or yield,
Or when to retreat and when to shield.
Yet I hesitate to let you shine,
For this bright world is not yet fine.
I'll keep your light for days unknown,
For times when seeds of hope are sown.
So, for now, I set you free,
To roam the earth, to sail the sea.
Live your life, and let it sing,
The melody of joy in everything.
I'll guard your dreams, both night and day,
With my blade's edge to clear the way.
But this vow, you'll never know,
As silently, I let you go.
I'll watch from shadows, far and near,
Protecting you from pain and fear.

And though I'll never speak of this,
I'll treasure the light your soul emits.
That tiny glow, so soft, so pure,
A beacon of hope, steadfast and sure.
It shines within, though you may not see,
The strength it gives to you and me.
The songs you sing, the path you tread,
The joy you spread, the dreams you've fed—
Each moment brings a gentle flame,
A spark of love I cannot name.
Go forth, dear soul, the world awaits,
With open arms and shifting fates.
Find your place, and claim your song,
Whether the journey is short or long.
Though I remain in the silent shade,
A steadfast guardian, unafraid.
My sword will guard the peace you seek,
A quiet strength, both firm and meek.
For even in this world's harshest fight,
I'll hold your dreams within my sight.
And when the time is right to soar,
You'll find the skies an open door.
Through you, I see the beauty unfurled,
A fleeting glimpse of a kinder world.
So, go, my star, let your light unfurl,
For you are my eyes, my heart, my pearl.

5. Dreams

Not every dream finds its wings to fly,
Not every soul calls a place home nearby.
We meet companions along the way,
But not every hand is there to stay.
Paths may cross, their lights may gleam,
But not every turn leads to the dream.
The bonds of hearts, so strange, so deep,
Not every love sows seeds we keep.
Some dreams linger within our sight,
Not every star shines through the night.
The boat of life sways in a restless tide,
Not every storm leaves dawn by its side.
Memories turn to shadows in the dark,
Not every morning ignites its spark.
Hopes bloom like flowers in the spring,
Not every garden hears the birds sing.
Sometimes solitude becomes a friend,
Not every gathering finds joy to lend.
We smile and hide the pain inside,
Not every tear is meant to be cried.
In this journey, all walk their course,
Not every traveller feels the same force.
Dreams remain etched in every mind,
Not every treasure is easy to find.

A sky of stars holds countless sights,
But not all constellations blaze in lights.
The heart holds wishes that seldom grow,
For not all seeds feel the rain's flow.
Yet dreams, they call us, night after night,
A whisper of hope in the quiet light.
For even when the world feels gray,
Dreams inspire, and show the way.
Though some paths end in silent despair,
Dreams teach us to persist, to dare.
Each turn, each fall, each fleeting glance,
Holds the promise of another chance.
In this world, so vast and wide,
Not every heart finds peace inside.
But still, we strive, we seek, we yearn,
For dreams give life at every turn.
Even when fate feels cruel and cold,
Dreams weave stories, new and bold.
Not every vision may come to be,
Yet dreams ignite eternity.
Through life's storms, we find our voice,
In every dream, there lies a choice.
To rise, to hope, to chase the gleam,
For life itself begins with a dream.

6. The Star That Never Shone

What kind of star hides its glow so deep,
Wrapped in the night, where shadows creep?
Its heart bears pain, yet no tears fall,
A silent struggler, enduring it all.
From afar, it seems like every star,
But up close, it fades, distant and far.
Its light confined to a dreamer's gaze,
In the real world, it's lost in haze.
Its sparkle once dreamed of skies untamed,
But fate held it back, unnamed, unclaimed.
A lonely beacon, companion of the night,
Shrouded in silence, a prisoner of plight.
Each whisper of darkness tells its tale,
A million hopes it failed to unveil.
The heavens vast couldn't make it whole,
For it carried a weight deep in its soul.
It longed to shine, to find its place,
But shadows bound it in a cruel embrace.
Through every dusk, its wishes grew,
Yet the dawn denied what it was due.
Beneath the stars that freely gleam,
It wandered alone, lost in a dream.
No joy it claimed, no brilliance found,
Just quiet despair, its only sound.

The winds would call, but it stayed still,
As if tethered by an unseen will.
It glimmered faint, in fleeting thought,
A spark of beauty the world forgot.
Once it hoped, its heart held fire,
To reach the heights of its own desire.
But destiny laughed and closed the door,
Leaving it stranded, longing for more.
Time wore on, the star grew dim,
Its radiance fading, edges grim.
A shadow now in the cosmic sea,
A trace of what it used to be.
At last, it fell, its light gave way,
Consumed by the night, it ceased to stay.
No longer a guide, no longer a flame,
Just a memory, without a name.
The sky no longer remembers its mark,
Its brilliance gone, extinguished spark.
It lives no more in tales of old,
Its story lost, its truth untold.
A star that dreamed, yet never could rise,
Bound by the weight of earthly ties.
It flickered out, unseen, unsung,
Its journey ended, its story spun.
In the endless void where dreams are sown,
Lies a forgotten star that never shone.
Though silent now, it whispers still,
A tale of hope, subdued by will.

And in its fall, a lesson lies,
For those who dare to touch the skies:
Though darkness looms, and shadows confine,
Each soul can rise, each star can shine.

7. The Tale of the Singing Deer

Upon a desolate, barren shore,
Lay a girl of royal blood and lore.
The waves whispered tales of her plight,
Shipwrecked alone in fading light.
No trees to shelter, no life in sight,
An island veiled in endless night.
Yet despair was not her lasting song,
For wonders waited, all along.
When the sun ascended, bold and bright,
And cast the seas in shimmering light,
From the ocean's depths they came,
Three singing deer of gentle frame.
They walked on waves, serene, aligned,
With steps so soft, no trail behind.
Upon their backs, a burden they bore,
Apples and cherries, a radiant store.
Their voices wove a melancholy tune,
Dancing beneath the blazing noon.
Across the vast and endless sea,
They journeyed on, steadfast and free.
At last, they reached the waiting land,
A tiny speck in a sea of sand.

The maiden watched with awe profound,
As they approached with measured sound.
Together they feasted on sunlit shores,
As laughter echoed, their spirits soared.
They danced to the tune of every song,
A fleeting world where none belonged.
As twilight spread its golden hue,
The flames rose high, the sky turned blue.
And when her eyes grew heavy with sleep,
They tucked her in with care so deep.
Under the stars, they watched her rest,
Guardians of a fate unexpressed.
Then, as the night began to wane,
They walked the waves, home again.
Into the horizon, they softly faded,
By moonlight's glow, serenely shaded.
Each day they'd return, with treasures to share,
A bond of magic beyond compare.
For though the island seemed cold and bare,
It thrived with wonder beyond despair.
And so the maiden found her peace,
Amidst the tides that never ceased.
Her story lingers, soft and clear,
Of the girl and the three singing deer.
A tale of hope on desolate sands,
Where miracles walk with gentle hands.
Across the sea, they venture still,
Bound by a promise, steadfast will.
Through sun and storm, they march along,

Carrying life, and a timeless song.
For even in the darkest days,
The heart finds light in wondrous ways.
And on that shore, where dreams appear,
Lives the legend of the singing deer.

8. An Invitation to the Divine

O mother so tender, so gracious, so kind,
Will you step into this humble shrine?
Adorn my home with your radiant glow,
Fill it with blessings that endlessly flow.
The floor is smeared with clay and dung,
Patterns etched with care, prayers sung.
Kumkum and rice flour form sacred designs,
A heartfelt welcome in delicate lines.
A trail of diyas softly alight,
Guides your path through the forest night.
Among the foliage, a hut does reside,
A haven of devotion where love abides.
For you, dear mother, I've prepared a feast,
With jalebis and barfis, a treat to eat.
Dishes so sweet, they'll make you smile,
Crafted with reverence, touched with style.
Come sit with me by the fire's warm glow,
On a mat of palms, where gratitude shows.
I'll sing you bhajans, my heart's melody,
Each note a prayer for serenity.
I ask for no gold, no land, no gain,
Just your darshan to ease my pain.
To celebrate, adore, and humbly pray,
For your blessing to guide me on my way.

Let this moment be eternal, divine,
Your presence turning the mundane to sublime.
A peaceful demise is all that I seek,
A final embrace, where souls softly speak.
Each diya burns with hope untold,
Each offering speaks of a story old.
Mother, your grace is the wealth I yearn,
To your eternal love, my spirit will turn.
Beneath this sky, where shadows blend,
Let your light guide until the end.
O mother, tender, so pure, so divine,
In this simple hut, let your glory shine.
A life of devotion, a heart made pure,
With your presence, I'll endure.
No riches could match this sacred plea—
Your darshan alone sets my spirit free.
By the fire's glow, we shall sit and sing,
Echoes of joy that the heavens will bring.
A bond of faith, unshaken and true,
This humble abode awaits only you.
With every word, my soul aligns,
With your love eternal, endlessly kind.
O mother, tender, in this fleeting life,
Grant me peace and release from strife.
For in your grace, all dreams ignite,
Your presence transforms the darkest night.
Come, O mother, in splendor divine,
This humble abode is forever thine.

9. The Mighty Hold of Jidayas

Behold the grip of Jidayas' might,

As he steers the reins of endless night.

Through the river of time, so vast and wide,

He plunges deep where shadows reside.

Into chaos, where the world is torn,

Yet emerges unscathed, though worn.

A figure in the storm, both fierce and scarred,

His spirit unbroken, though life is hard.

A thousand years, a thousand more,

He stands unchanged on the forgotten shore.

Rugged, ruthless, his soul unmanned,

He holds his ground with an iron hand.

On the edge of time, he makes his stand,

A silhouette etched upon the land.

Ready to face the foes ahead,

As a guardian to the life once led.

A cherub of fate, a sentinel bold,

Who guards the path where secrets are told.

The tree of life, so ancient and still,

That bears no fruit, yet stands on the hill.

It endures through the ages, unyielding and wise,

Beneath ever-changing, eternal skies.

Jidayas stands, with resolve so true,
A force that time itself cannot undo.
Though chaos swarms and the earth may quake,
His purpose remains, for honor's sake.
Onward he marches, through flame and ice,
A sentinel at the threshold of sacrifice.
The tree of life, in silence it weeps,
For the fruits it's yet to keep.
But Jidayas, unwavering, guards its boughs,
A sentinel enduring through all that allows.
He watches the passage, through ages unseen,
A keeper of secrets, where none have been.
The passage remains, from dawn to dusk,
Guarded by Jidayas, in him we trust.
A warrior of fate, in the fabric of time,
His steps resonate like an ancient rhyme.
As he treads the path where none dare follow,
A champion of light, in darkness so hollow.
Through aeons he stands, unmoving, unshaken,
A witness to lives that have been forsaken.
The tree remains barren, yet still it grows,
As Jidayas endures, where only he knows.
For though no fruit blooms on the tree,
Its roots run deep, as deep as can be.
And Jidayas stands, a guardian still,
Fulfilling his purpose with unwavering will.
So behold the might of Jidayas' grace,
As he surfs the tides, in time's embrace.
Ruthless and rugged, yet steadfast he stays,

On the threshold of eternity, through all of his days.

10. A Christmas Miracle

On this special Christmas night,
I lit a candle, soft and bright,
Placed it gently on the table,
And thought upon the timeless fable.
A miracle, I pondered then,
A story told by humble men—
Born in a stable, cold and bare,
A King of kings, beyond compare.
Emmanuel, the worthy One,
Underneath the bright star's sun.
A humble birth, a holy sight,
To bring the world its guiding light.
For in that manger, on that day,
A Savior came, to light the way.
To burn upon the cross, so high,
To lift us up, to purify.
A gift of love, a gift so pure,
To heal the hearts, and hearts endure.
He came to teach, to show the way,
To bring us peace on Christmas Day.
And as I sat there in the glow,
The candle's flame, so soft and low,
I thought of how the light does shine,
In every heart, a spark divine.

Through every storm and darkest night,
That humble birth brings endless light.
A love so vast, it knows no end,
A message that will never bend.
For born that night, so long ago,
A king of kings, with love aglow.
He came to heal, to love, to save,
And guide us all beyond the grave.
His light still shines through every soul,
A beacon bright, that makes us whole.
And though He walked the path of pain,
His love remains, our hearts to claim.
So let this Christmas, in our hearts,
The miracle of love restart.
To burn with kindness, peace, and grace,
And let His light fill every place.
For on this night, we understand,
The worth of love, the Savior's hand.
To burn upon the cross, so free,
To bring His light to you and me.
A Christmas gift, so pure and bright,
To shine forever, day and night.
And as we sit in peace and prayer,
We know His love is everywhere.
So let this flame within us burn,
And guide us always, as we learn,
That on that Christmas, long ago,
A King was born, to make us whole.

In every heart, His light we find,
To heal, to lift, and to remind,
That Christmas is a time to see,
The miracle of love, eternally.

11. The Tale of the Meadow

Two goats and three cows,
Sat on a meadow one fine day,
They chewed on grass,
And savored some hay.
They gazed at the sky,
Counting the birds in flight,
While a lonesome buffalo,
Puffed smoke from a broken pipe.
The goats, with curious eyes,
Turned to the cows and said,
"Have you been to the land,
Beyond the moon, where dreams are fed?
Where the sky is clear,
And the grass is maroon,
Where the sun is bright,
And the stars shine like a boon?"
The cows, in a voice so calm,
Said in unison, so true,
"Yes, dear, we've been there,
To that land of yellow and maroon.
A place where knights and kings,
And ladies fair and queens,
Walk gently like us,
With hearts pure and serene.

They move with grace,
On all four, just like us,
And in their land of beauty,
No need for hurry or fuss.
They roam through meadows,
Where the grass is rich and deep,
And when the day turns twilight,
They chew cud in peaceful sleep.
A place of joy, of peace and rest,
Where all are treated the best,
Where laughter flows like a stream,
And every day is like a dream."
The goats, their eyes wide with wonder,
Nodded slowly, taking in the tale.
The buffalo puffed one more time,
As the meadow filled with a gentle gale.
And so the goats and cows,
Sat in quiet, thinking deep,
Of lands beyond the sky so blue,
Where dreams and meadows softly sweep.
For in their hearts, a wish did grow,
To see the land beyond the glow,
Where knights and queens and kings may roam,
And all creatures find a peaceful home.
But for now, they chewed their grass,
And savored every bite,
Content with the meadow,
Under the stars so bright.

And though they longed for distant lands,
They knew the meadow was their home,
Where grass was green, and hay was sweet,
And they would never be alone.

12. The Daughters of Zion and the Stranger

Stranger:

"O daughters fair of Zion's land,

Why do you wander o'er the shifting sand?

When noon is ripe, the sun's embrace,

For a cozy slumber, in a shaded space."

Daughters of Zion:

"Hark, O stranger, heed our tale,

You who ride the winged stallion's sail.

Fly away, don't linger here,

Or ponder on what you hold dear.

We seek not celery, nor corn, nor spice,

Nor saffron from a lofty place so nice.

We follow the quails that glide on high,

To nourish those who suffer and cry.

We feed the lepers who rest and weep,

On the outskirts, where the shadows creep.

By day they brood, by night they sing,

And glorify the One who'll yet bring

Hope to the hopeless, though late it seems,

But never forgetting, He fulfills their dreams.

Though the world may overlook their plight,

He will come to them in the darkest night.

We serve them with joy, though weary we be,
For in their plight, we find our plea.
Our journey, though long, has no regret,
For we know our cause, and we won't forget.
So fly on, O stranger, if you must go,
But know the lepers in their sorrow will grow.
And we, the daughters, who walk this way,
Will keep on seeking, come night or day."
Stranger:
"I see your path is one of grace,
A noble cause that none can replace.
Though my journey leads me far and wide,
I'll carry your message with me, side by side."
And with that, the stranger spread his wings,
And soared above, as the golden bell rings.
The daughters of Zion, with hearts so pure,
Continue their journey, steadfast and sure.
For their mission is one of love and care,
To heal the broken, to be always there.
Through desert sands and endless night,
They spread the hope of a promised light.

13. O Werewolves of the Night

O werewolves of the night,
When the moon ascends to its silvery height,
Grace my threshold with your howling cry,
But bring no terror to the shadows nearby.
With blood-smeared fangs and fiery eyes aglow,
You carry a beauty only the daring know.
A sight of ferocity, primal and grand,
Crafted by nature's untamed hand.
The moonlit stage is yours to claim,
A dance of the wild, untamed flame.
Your snarls echo through the midnight air,
A chilling song, yet beyond compare.
Your mesmerizing transition, fierce and true,
Beneath the moonlight's argent hue.
Bones shift and twist in a haunting ballet,
Man becomes beast as night turns day.
The whispers of the forest hush in awe,
As claws emerge from a once-human paw.
The power within you is raw, unchained,
A mystery of flesh and spirit sustained.
O creatures bound to lunar decree,
What secrets lie within thee?

Do you remember the man you were?
Or does the wolf in you now deter?
The blaze in your eyes tells tales untold,
Of ancient curses and legends old.
Fangs that gleam like polished steel,
Mark the predator beneath the zeal.
I do not fear, but yearn to see,
The raw, untamed ferocity.
Though frightful it may seem to some,
I wait for the werewolf's hour to come.
When the moon rides high in the sable sea,
And the world succumbs to nocturnity,
Your shadow stalks the earth below,
A phantom presence, silent yet aglow.
The thrill of your power, the grace of your stride,
A dance of the wild you cannot hide.
Even in terror, your beauty shines,
Like a forbidden fruit on ancient vines.
O werewolf, do you curse the moon?
Do you yearn for its rise, or beg its tune?
Is the beast your bane or your reprieve?
A burdened gift or a cruel deceive?
Do you hunt with malice or hunger's plea?
Do you pine for a life of simplicity?
O werewolves of the shadowed night,
What dwells within your heart's plight?
But I ask not for the answers, no,
For your haunting visage is all I know.
When the moon's high nation commands your shape,

I'll behold the magic, the primal escape.
Even as terror grips the lands,
Your power stirs like ancient sands.
O frightful sight, magnificent and vast,
A glimpse of legends from ages past.
You are both the dream and the despair,
The silent growl in the midnight air.
In your essence lies a paradox true,
Beauty in the wild, the old, and the new.
O werewolves of the night, arise!
Under the moon, claim the skies.
Though fearsome, you are a wondrous sight,
A haunting muse in the pale moonlight.
So come to my door, but strike no fear,
Your bloodied fangs and blazing eyes, clear.
For though the sight might chill the bone,
It's a glimpse of a world not my own.
The primal echoes of your haunting howl,
Stir the soul and make the spirit growl.
And though your claws may mark the ground,
In your curse, a strange beauty is found.
For the frightful sight you bring to bear,
Is a feast for eyes beyond compare.
O werewolves of the mystic night,
Yours is the kingdom of silver light.
So let the moon ascend its throne,
And let your transformation be known.
For in the shadows of your wild refrain,
I find the beauty within the pain.

14. A Symphony of Life

Life can be a gentle stream,
Flowing softly, like a dream.
Devoid of weights, free from care,
If only you learn what to hold and where.
To know the art of letting go,
And when to let your passions flow.
To seize the day, embrace the sun,
While light and warmth have just begun.
When skies are clear, make your hay,
Prepare for storms that may cloud the day.
And when the rains begin to pour,
Find joy within, let your spirit soar.
Create some gravy, taste the sweet,
Dance to the rhythm of life's beat.
Savor the savory, embrace the spice,
Find the flavor in sacrifice.
Don't count your days in toil alone,
Or weigh the seeds that you have sown.
Instead, recount the joys you've spent,
Moments of laughter, fully lent.
Life isn't measured by the grind,
But by the treasures your heart can find.
Count not the spoil, but the delight,
That turns your darkness into light.

Like a lark in morning's song,
Let your happiness carry you along.
With wings of freedom, rise and soar,
And find new skies forevermore.
Fill your days with melodies sweet,
Symphonies of joy at your feet.
Let cymbals clash and chimes resound,
In your heart where dreams are found.
A goblet of sherry in your hand,
Toast to the life you've bravely planned.
For the smile you wear will light the years,
A testament to conquered fears.
The signature upon your face,
A glowing mark of time's embrace.
A radiant proof of a life well-spent,
Each wrinkle a story, each line a vent.
Life's glory lies in moments small,
The laughter shared, the rise and fall.
The simple joy of a fleeting breeze,
Or sunlight dancing through the trees.
It's found in kindness softly spoken,
In bonds of love that stay unbroken.
In lessons learned through storm and flame,
Each trial a step toward the aim.
Hold tight to those who lift your soul,
And let go of what you can't control.
For life's too short to bear the weight,
Of every sorrow or twist of fate.

Relinquish grudges, free your mind,
In forgiveness, peace you'll find.
The years will stretch with ease and grace,
When love and joy leave their trace.
So, sing like the lark at dawn's first light,
Revel in the day, cherish the night.
Let symphonies echo through the vale,
A chorus of triumph, a jubilant tale.
The smile you wear becomes your art,
A masterpiece of a glowing heart.
An emblem of joy, a radiant gleam,
A life that mirrors a golden dream.
For every year that gently turns,
Is a candle bright, a flame that burns.
And in its glow, your story lives,
A life that thrives, a soul that gives.
So take these days, both brief and grand,
And sculpt a life with your own hand.
Relish the savory, toast the sweet,
Dance to the rhythm, feel the beat.
Life is a song, a tune sublime,
A fleeting note in the hands of time.
Let your melody sing, your joy take flight,
And fill your world with radiant light.
For when the journey's at its end,
And to the stars your soul ascends,
The echoes of your laughter clear,
Will linger on, forever near.

15. Woe of a Wounded Knight

The horsemen of Kondo, fierce and proud,
Watch me now from their mountain shroud.
Eyes like embers, sharp and keen,
They wait in shadows, cold and mean.
But I have walked where legends tread,
And spilled the blood their fears once fed.
For while their spears have met with strife,
I carved my name with the blade of life.
They dream of glory, yet taste despair,
While I stand crowned in the fire's glare.
My wounds may bleed, but never weep,
For my perfect sweep they could not reap.
Old and tattered, their spirits wane,
They mourn their dead with silent pain.
No mortal desire, no question asked,
Will lead them here, where shadows basked.
They claimed the throne through hollow might,
But I am the king, forged in fire's light.
My eyes are wrapped in sapphire gleam,
A treasure bound to my own dream.
No heir shall rise to take my place,
For I am the keeper of time and space.

Their lineage falters, a fleeting lore,
While I endure, forevermore.
My wounds bathe in ancient brine,
A sacred blend of the oceans' spine.
From Kardos Rest, where tides entwine,
I find a strength both fierce and divine.
The salt renews, the pain subsides,
While ancient whispers with me abide.
I bear the scars, the knight's lament,
A life of toil, yet never spent.
Oh, if I could unwind the clock,
To days when silence veiled their talk.
When in their mothers' wombs they lay,
Unshaped by greed, untouched by day.
I'd keep them still, deny their birth,
Prevent the blight that haunts this earth.
No smile would grace their youthful face,
Nor would their shadows this world disgrace.
But time marches on, and fate remains,
A cruel reminder of endless chains.
Yet here I stand, defiant and bold,
While they decay in their mountain's cold.
The horsemen of Kondo cannot see,
The depths of power inside of me.
For while they falter, bound by stone,
I rise, unyielding, utterly alone.
Their swords may gleam, their banners fly,
But none can match my burning eye.
It holds the fire, the wrath untamed,

The ancient force that none have claimed.
Let them whisper of vengeance near,
I'll answer back with no trace of fear.
For every blow they strike in vain,
Will be met with wrath they cannot sustain.
The mountains echo their hollow cries,
But I remain, where honor lies.
No trembling voice, no pleading sigh,
Shall break the will of a knight so high.
So come, O horsemen, take your chance,
Let the swords clash in a deadly dance.
But know this truth, I shall not fall,
For I am the fire that consumes them all.
Their lineage fades, their kingdom dies,
While I rise anew beneath the skies.
Crowned not by men, but by the flame,
Eternal keeper of glory's name.
So woe to me, a knight so scarred,
By battles fought and bodies marred.
Yet even in sorrow, I find my reign,
A timeless king, born of fire and pain.
The horsemen of Kondo watch and wait,
But I have defied both death and fate.
With sapphire eyes and wounds of brine,
I tread a path forever mine.
For though my heart bears loss untold,
It burns within, relentless, bold.
And in the end, when shadows creep,
It's my fire that will never sleep.

16. The Actor's Creed

Do not linger, silent and still,
In this world of chaos, joy, and will.
A realm of mirth, where sorrow lies,
A stage where hopes and dreams arise.
Be not a watcher in the crowd,
Hidden in shadows, silent, bowed.
Step forth, take your place in the light,
Be it dawn's embrace or the fall of night.
The world's a stage, the roles diverse,
A king's command, or a pauper's curse.
Whatever the script, let it unfold,
With courage fierce and a spirit bold.
Play your part, and play it true,
Whether skies are gray or painted blue.
Let every word, each gesture told,
Reflect a heart both pure and bold.
No need for masks, no guise of lies,
For truth endures when falsehood dies.
Each act, each scene, a fleeting thread,
A tapestry woven till life is shed.
Be not afraid to stumble or fall,
For errors shape the greatest of all.
Even in failure, the lesson shines,
Guiding the soul through endless lines.

The pauper's cloak may weigh you down,
But wear it with grace, not with a frown.
The crown of a king may dazzle bright,
But burdens it bears oft dim the light.
For every role, both great and small,
Has worth and meaning that shapes us all.
It's not the stature, wealth, or fame,
But the truth in your heart that stakes your claim.
So tread the boards with steady stride,
Let passion be your only guide.
Through joy and sorrow, rise and fall,
Embrace the story that binds us all.
The stage may shift, the lights may dim,
The chorus fade to a solemn hymn.
Yet the echoes of your voice remain,
A melody sung through joy and pain.
Do not seek applause or cheers,
For fleeting are such mortal gears.
Instead, seek meaning, deep and vast,
A legacy that forever lasts.
Be it a king with robes of gold,
Or a pauper whose tale is quietly told.
Each role, unique, has something to say,
A truth to share, a price to pay.
The actor's craft is not to deceive,
But to inspire, to make hearts believe.
To show the beauty in the strife,
To breathe new meaning into life.

Play your part with all your might,
Let your soul burn with radiant light.
For at the end, when curtains close,
It's the story told that truly shows.
The crowd may scatter, the stage grow bare,
But your truth will linger in the air.
The echo of your lines will ring,
A timeless song that spirits sing.
So step into the chaos, the mirth, the lore,
And be the actor, forevermore.
Whether joy or pain, let your story be,
A beacon of hope for all to see.
The world awaits, the stage is set,
No act too small, no role to regret.
For the greatest play is simply this:
To live with purpose, and not to miss.
Do not stand idle, mere spectator,
Be the dreamer, the creator.
The actor who plays with heart and soul,
Fulfilling the universe's endless role.
At the day's end, when the lights turn low,
When the final act is all you know,
You'll find the journey was worth the cost,
No scene forgotten, no line was lost.
So heed the call, and take your place,
With steadfast courage, infinite grace.
For every part is yours to own,
And every truth, a seed that's sown.

Be not a shadow, pale and meek,
But a flame that burns, unique, antique.
In this world of chaos, love, and lore,
Be the actor, forevermore.

17. The Eternal Question

Is this the purpose of life, so frail,
To love and be loved, and yet to fail?
To break apart, then let it go,
A cycle endless, we scarcely know.
To share, to care, to laugh, to cry,
To watch the days and nights pass by.
To toil by day and rest by night,
And chase the dawn with fading might.
What purpose does this life behold,
In stories told and truths retold?
Why kings are rich but hearts are bare,
While paupers dance with naught to spare.
Is happiness found in golden thrones,
Or in the whispers of simple tones?
Do treasures fill the void within,
Or is joy the fruit of lives thin?
For kings may feast and still despair,
While paupers find joy in humble fare.
What meaning lies in wealth or fame,
If hearts are empty, all the same?
The stars above, the earth below,
Hold secrets vast we cannot know.
The oceans roar, the mountains rise,
Yet still we ask beneath the skies:

What binds the soul to flesh and bone?
What path will lead us to our home?
Is it love, or toil, or fleeting grace,
That gives our fleeting lives their place?
When all has ended, when time has flown,
And we stand at gates of the great unknown,
Do we carry with us the deeds we've done,
Or the love we've shared beneath the sun?
The pauper laughs, the king may weep,
Yet both are bound for eternal sleep.
When the curtain falls, and the tale is spun,
Are we all the same, the many, the one?
Do we strive for glory, for power, for pride,
Or seek the truth where hearts abide?
Is purpose found in what we achieve,
Or in the moments we simply believe?
Perhaps it's not for us to find,
A single truth to ease the mind.
Perhaps life's purpose shifts and bends,
With every chapter, until it ends.
A fleeting joy, a sorrow's tear,
A whisper soft, a memory near.
Each moment shapes the life we lead,
A patchwork quilt of thought and deed.
So why do kings feel hollow inside,
While paupers find peace in their humble stride?
Is it the weight of the crown they bear,
Or the freedom found in a life laid bare?

DO WE LIVE, OR JUST EXIST?

The stars will shine, the rivers flow,
But life's true meaning we may not know.
Is it in loving, in giving, in letting go,
Or in the seeds of kindness we quietly sow?
When we pack to go, beyond the door,
To the realm where time exists no more,
What will we take, and what will remain,
When life's sweet joys are met with pain?
Perhaps the purpose is not a goal,
But the journey walked by every soul.
To love, to lose, to learn, to grow,
To embrace the highs and endure the lows.
For kings and paupers, all the same,
Will leave behind their earthly name.
No crown of gold, no beggar's plea,
Will matter when we cease to be.
So cherish the moments, fleeting, rare,
The bonds we form, the love we share.
For in the end, when life's threads sever,
Perhaps it's those that last forever.
What purpose life holds, we may never find,
A riddle vast, a question unkind.
Yet in the asking, in the quest we strive,
Perhaps therein lies the purpose of life.
So hold the question, let it burn,
With every step, with every turn.
For life itself, in all its strife,
Might simply be the purpose of life.

18. A Singular Creation

Fuel your mind with vivid thought,
Imagination's fire, so fiercely wrought.
Let no vague indignation cloud the way,
For you are a marvel, born of clay.
A single piece, unique, untamed,
A soul unmatched, no twin proclaimed.
Crafted fine by unseen hands,
A wonder walking earthly lands.
No duplication shadows your grace,
No other form can take your place.
You stand alone, a masterpiece,
Your essence roaring, never at peace.
Live as a king, with crown unseen,
Your throne the earth, your robe the green.
Though no sovereign nation bears your name,
Your spirit shines with royal flame.
Life's not about the treasures won,
But moments lived, one by one.
Each breath, a spark; each step, a song,
A fleeting dance where we belong.
Let intentions guide, both clear and true,
In all you seek, in all you do.
Yet temptations call, with whispers sweet,
A siren's song to hearts they greet.

The stars above may light the night,
But your soul burns with brighter might.
For you are the cosmos, bound in skin,
The universe folds itself within.
A coronation awaits each day,
With every dawn, a kingly sway.
No golden crown, no silken throne,
Yet regal, you stand—your path your own.
Do not chase shadows, fleeting, vain,
For glory fades like summer rain.
Instead, hold fast to moments pure,
Where joy and love forever endure.
Be the sun that warms the cold,
A light that shines, both brave and bold.
Be the river, winding free,
Carving paths to destiny.
Temptations lure with gilded charm,
But wield your will to disarm.
For life is not a fleeting chase,
But a steady stride, a measured pace.
The world is vast, with wonders grand,
Yet you're the treasure, close at hand.
No mountain high, no ocean wide,
Can match the magic found inside.
Each moment whispers, soft, profound,
In every heart, life's pulse resounds.
A tapestry woven with threads of gold,
A story unique, a tale untold.

So rise, creation, bold and true,
The world awaits the light of you.
With every breath, embrace your fate,
A timeless spark in life's estate.
The skies may darken, storms may rise,
But hold your ground; you're no disguise.
Your heart, a compass, fierce and wise,
Will guide you through the endless skies.
Be tempted not by fleeting fame,
For life's true wealth is in the name.
Not etched in stone or sung in lore,
But in the lives you've touched and more.
Moments build the grand parade,
Brick by brick, the path is laid.
With clear intent, and heart's elation,
You are the marvel of creation.
The kingly life, it is your own,
Even without a sovereign throne.
For wealth and power pale in face,
Of the joy you bring to time and space.
So take your crown, it's always been,
A symbol not of pride, but kin.
You're one of many, yet stand alone,
A masterpiece the world has known.
Life whispers softly, "Take your place,
Within this wondrous, boundless space."
Live moments fully, tempt the stars,
And bear your light, despite the scars.

The world is yours to shape, to claim,
With every step, rekindle flame.
And when the final act is played,
You'll know your mark will never fade.
A singular creation, you shall remain,
No duplicate to share your name.
For you are more than fleeting breath,
A soul transcending life and death.
Live, creation, vivid, free,
A force of nature, destiny.
Moments pass, but you'll inspire,
A timeless spark, eternal fire.

19. The Canvas of Conflicted Skies

The clouds above began their play,
A thousand lambs in wild array.
Across the heavens, they danced, they spun,
Casting shadows beneath the noonday sun.
Their shapes would shift, then blend anew,
A fleeting art on the canvas blue.
No steady hand could chart their flight,
A restless gallery, born of light.
Each form they took, a story told,
Of dreams half-formed, and thoughts grown cold.
A critic's hand, uncertain, bound,
Tracing lines where no truth was found.
Confusion whispered in every curve,
A faltering stroke, a trembling nerve.
The artist's mind a tempest vast,
Lost in the echoes of the past.
The heart it bore was pierced and torn,
A vessel for grief long forlorn.
It longed to paint with vibrant hue,
Yet shadows bled into every view.
No sunlit meadow graced the frame,
No triumph bold, no fleeting fame.

The brush would drift, its rhythm break,
As if the soul itself might quake.
For in the depths of the artist's chest,
A sorrow lingered, unconfessed.
A tale it sought to shun, evade,
Yet haunted every stroke it made.
The clouds above, in mimicry,
Reflected this same dichotomy.
Bright edges lit by golden flame,
Yet shadows followed, just the same.
And so the sky became a stage,
Where heart and hand could silently rage.
Each wisp, a thought unspoken, lost,
Each gust, a sigh for bridges crossed.
The critic's heart, though burdened, yearned,
For peace in lessons never learned.
Yet the tale it carried, sharp and deep,
Was one the skies could only weep.
The lambs of mischief danced away,
Yet shadows stretched and chose to stay.
They lingered long, in shapes unclear,
A mirror to the artist's fear.
And still, the canvas held its hue,
Both radiant gold and brooding blue.
A masterpiece of light and dark,
A testament to the artist's mark.
No tale was told, no truth complete,
Yet in the chaos lay something sweet.
For even sorrow holds its grace,

When brushed by time in soft embrace.
So clouds may wander, skies may shift,
And hearts may drift, bereft of gift.
But in their passage, art is born,
A solace for the soul forlorn.
O critic of the canvas vast,
Your pain is ink, your grief will last.
Yet in its depth, a beauty lies,
Reflected in the painted skies.
For even shadows bear their worth,
When cast upon the light of earth.
And every tale, though sharp it stings,
Can lend its voice to angel's wings.
The lambs disperse, the sky turns grey,
But still, your heart will find its way.
A painter torn, yet still you stand,
A brush of sorrow in trembling hand.
The clouds above move on, set free,
A mirror to your artistry.
So let them drift, as thoughts will do,
A fleeting gallery, ever new.

20. Eternal Whisper: A Dialogue with Sleep

O night, so deep, a velvet sea,

Your darkness wraps and comforts me.

The breeze, a balm, so soft, so kind,

It soothes the ache within my mind.

The silence speaks, a tender plea,

A whispered call, "Come, rest with me."

Unveil yourself, step from the shade,

I hear your voice, I am not afraid.

Your touch, so light, a fragile grace,

A ghostly hand, a sweet embrace.

From cradle days, you've lingered near,

A quiet presence, always clear.

Through childhood's dreams and fleeting wiles,

You watched me with your shadowed smiles.

When tears would fall, when fears would grow,

Your tender strokes would soothe the woe.

By night you call, by day I stray,

For life's demands do lead away.

But know, sweet sleep, I've not betrayed,

Your love remains, though I've delayed.

The time is young, the world still spins,

I chase my days through thick and thin.

Yet in my heart, your promise lies,
A comfort deep beneath the skies.
One day, I know, the time will cease,
And I will find eternal peace.
Your arms will open, soft and wide,
And I'll return, no need to hide.
No fear shall linger, no pain will stay,
As you and I drift far away.
To lands unknown, where shadows gleam,
And stars illuminate the dream.
Your voice, so quiet, always near,
Will sing me songs I long to hear.
A lullaby of endless rest,
A final home within your chest.
So wait for me, O loving sleep,
Your promises I vow to keep.
Till life has spent its fleeting fire,
And all that's left is your desire.
Your whispers grow, though faint they be,
A melody that calls to me.
But I shall wait, for life's not done,
There's more to feel beneath the sun.
Yet when the final twilight falls,
And every fleeting moment calls,
I'll walk to you, with open arms,
And find my peace in all your charms.
Together, then, no parting pain,
No days to lose, no nights in vain.
Eternity shall be our keep,

Forever bound, in loving sleep.
So hush, dear whisper, soft and slow,
The time will come, and I will know.
Till then, remain, a patient shade,
A promise in the dark, well laid.
For when my soul grows tired and worn,
And all my earthly ties are torn,
I'll seek your arms, your quiet grace,
And find my final resting place.
Eternal sleep, my faithful friend,
Our story waits a gentle end.
Till then, O love, in shadows deep,
I bid you wait, my loving sleep.

21. At the Edge of Worlds: A Retiree's Reverie

If the world were but a boundless line,
And the sky an orb, a sphere divine,
I'd find my place where both do meet,
At horizons vast, where dreams compete.
There I'd settle, with heart at ease,
Beneath a mahogany's timeless leaves.
A weathered chair, cabriole and worn,
Would cradle me through nights and morn.
A talking dog, my steadfast friend,
Would share with me tales that never end.
A bunny, small and always sly,
Would hop around with a twinkling eye.
We'd sit together, this merry crew,
Beneath the skies of changing hues.
I'd light a fire with a gentle glow,
Its embers warm, its flicker slow.
And from my lap, my golden lyre,
Would sing of days that never tire.
The meadow's dance would join in tune,
Under the gaze of the watching moon.
There I'd brood, but not with grief,
Just thoughtful sighs, a soft relief.

For life has passed, both swift and sure,
Yet left me wisdom, vast and pure.
The "lang syne" plays its tender notes,
Through memory's seas, my mind still floats.
Each wave a moment, sharp or sweet,
Each crest a soul I once did meet.
Time's touch has made me worn, yet sage,
A story etched on every page.
Senescence lingers, a gentle friend,
Whispering truths that will not bend.
A penny's worth of cunning gained,
Through life's odd tricks, through joys and pains.
I seek no solace, no pity's grace,
For this, my world, is my chosen place.
Lonely? Perhaps, but not bereft,
For in this life, much joy is left.
The company of a quirky pair,
A dog that talks, a bunny rare.
The breeze that whispers through the leaves,
The fire's crackle, the tune it weaves.
The distant stars, their quiet gleam,
The boundless space to sit and dream.
Each day unfolds with its own charm,
Each night enfolds me, safe and warm.
The fantasies I conjure here,
Replace the noise, dissolve the fear.
For who can grieve when life is this—
A world of wonder, a state of bliss?
No crowded halls, no ceaseless din,

Just nature's hymn, my soul within.
At the edge of worlds, I take my stand,
With heart unburdened, a steady hand.
I need no more than this sweet spot,
For here I have all that life forgot.
So leave me be, in this retreat,
Where time and space as one do meet.
Let others chase the fleeting mirth,
I'll stay content on this humble earth.
For though the world may pass me by,
And others seek their mountaintop high,
I've found my peace, my final tune,
Beneath the sun and the watchful moon.
Let the horizon stretch afar,
Let dreams align with every star.
I'll sit and strum my golden lyre,
Beside my fire, my heart's desire.
And when the days grow short at last,
And all the moments fade to past,
I'll leave this place with gentle pride,
Knowing I lived where worlds collide.
A fantasy? Perhaps, it's true,
But it's the life I long to pursue.
To sit and dream, to laugh, to sing,
To live as freely as the spring.
At the edge of worlds, I'll make my mark,
A quiet soul, a steady spark.
For I may be lonely, but never bereft,
In my world of wonder, I'm richly blessed.

22. The Road's Call to Freedom

The lonely road, a silent guide,
Whispers softly, "Come, abide.
Hasten forth, let feet take flight,
Embrace the path, forsake the night."
Its voice, a song, both firm and kind,
A call to leave the past behind.
"Trudge along, do not retreat,
Each step forward makes you complete.
Leave aside the weight you bear,
The memories woven with love and care.
For though they comfort, though they glow,
They tether you where winds won't blow.
Cast away the chains of desire,
The fleeting sparks that hearts inspire.
Love, passion, goals you hold,
Are gilded cages, bright yet cold.
They shine, they burn, they tempt the soul,
But leave behind an empty hole.
For glory waits where few will go,
Beyond the bounds of all you know.
The road curves on, unseen, unknown,
A path that's yours and yours alone.

Its twists and turns may seem unkind,
But there, your truth you'll surely find.
Do not linger, do not stall,
For stagnant hearts can never call.
Break free from bonds of fleeting joy,
That tether dreams and lives destroy.
The road's own song is wild and free,
A hymn of endless mystery.
Its voice, a wind that cuts through stone,
Declares, "You are not meant to moan.
You're meant to soar, to reach, to climb,
To taste the edge of space and time.
Your solemn joy lies not in rest,
But in the quest, the unceasing quest."
Each step you take, a story grows,
A map of wonders no one knows.
The skies will stretch, the stars will gleam,
As you pursue your boundless dream.
No bonds of love should hold you tight,
No passion dim your guiding light.
No lofty goals should chain your wings,
For freedom's tune is what life sings.
The road will test, will make you strong,
Its trials fierce, its journey long.
But in each stride, a gift you'll find,
A clearer heart, a freer mind.
What lies ahead, no one can say,
Each dawn will bring a brand-new day.
And though the past may softly weep,

The future calls, a voice to keep.
The road is patient, always near,
Its whispers bold, its message clear.
"Come, wanderer, abandon fear,
For glory's trail lies far from here.
Your heart may ache, your body tire,
But step by step, you'll climb much higher.
Through forests deep, through mountains vast,
Through rivers swift, your will is cast.
The world is waiting, wild and wide,
A boundless book, its pages untried.
So walk, and write your story there,
Among the winds, beyond despair.
Do not let comfort's fleeting hand,
Chain you to the shifting sand.
For joy that's real, for peace that stays,
Lies only in the untamed ways.
The lonely road, your faithful guide,
Will stand with you, where dreams collide.
Each step you take, it will remain,
A silent partner through joy and pain.
So hasten now, and heed the call,
Forsake the ties that bind you small.
The road is waiting, long and free,
Come wanderer, it beckons thee."

23. A Drift Upon the Endless Sea

Life's a boat on the ocean wide,
A vessel frail, with dreams as guide.
It floats upon the waves serene,
A fleeting speck on waters green.
It may sail with a steady breeze,
Through calm expanses, beneath tall trees.
The stars above, its compass bright,
A beacon in the quiet night.
It may toss when tempests roar,
As thunder claps and waters pour.
Each surge a trial, each wave a test,
Yet onward still, it finds its quest.
It may trail, slow and unsure,
Through currents dark and paths obscure.
Drifting softly, lost in thought,
Seeking meaning, answers sought.
For every course it dares to chart,
The ocean mirrors the beating heart.
Its depths unknown, its surface vast,
A tale of now and echoes past.
But should it touch the waiting shore,
And seek to journey nevermore,

Its purpose wanes, its spirit fades,
Its sails retire to still cascades.
For life's not meant to rest and bind,
Nor cling to safety, deaf and blind.
It thrives in movement, in open space,
In winds that carry to each new place.
The coast may call with siren's tune,
A promise sweet beneath the moon.
Yet fleeting joy, a gilded snare,
Leaves the soul restless, longing elsewhere.
Each wave a lesson, each tide a choice,
A whisper soft, the ocean's voice.
"Do not linger, do not cease,
For in the motion, lies your peace."
The winds may shift, the skies may weep,
The sea may swell with secrets deep.
But life's a boat, its essence free,
Meant to wander the endless sea.
It's not the harbor that marks the gain,
But the journey's tale, the joy, the pain.
The distant shores, the unseen land,
The dance of oars, the guiding hand.
So set the sail and seize the gale,
Let the spirit roam, let the heart prevail.
Through storm or calm, through joy or dread,
The open sea is where life's led.
Do not anchor to what you know,
For the ocean's gift is to let you grow.
Each horizon holds a mystery vast,

A future bold, a treasure cast.
The waves will lift, the tides will turn,
The sun will set, the stars will burn.
And as the boat drifts far from shore,
Its purpose found, forevermore.
For life's a journey, not a place,
A boundless song, a ceaseless race.
And those who float with courage free,
Find their truth upon the sea.
Though ports may tempt with comfort's hand,
It's the ocean's vastness that understands,
That life's true calling, wild and grand,
Is to seek, to sail, to take a stand.
So let the boat, with heart unbound,
Ride the waves, where dreams are found.
For in the endless, open scene,
Life finds its truth on the ocean green.

24. The Bard on the Battlefield

The world stands still, as if in dread,
A haunting silence cloaks the dead.
The air is thick with sorrow's weight,
A battlefield, a twisted fate.
I do not know the reason why
The women mourn, yet warriors die.
Their tears fall fast for lives undone,
Yet clash they do beneath the sun.
What talisman do I now bear,
To walk amidst such deep despair?
What omen must I humbly seek,
To hear the answers spirits speak?
The angels, silent, watch me roam,
Through lands that once were called my home.
They do not rise, they do not call,
And yet I feel their shadows fall.
Why firmly am I bound to stone,
A witness here, but not alone?
Each step I take, the echoes moan,
Through bones of men, through blood-soaked loam.
I've sung of kings and glories vast,
Of battles won, of moments past.

But now my song is fraught with pain,
For honor lost and lives in vain.
The days of old rise in the haze,
A fleeting glimpse of gentler days.
When fields were green, and rivers clear,
Now stained with grief and lasting fear.
My time of honor draws so near,
Its voice resounds, yet strikes with fear.
For bards must bear the weight of truth,
The tales of age, the dreams of youth.
I wander now through realms of strife,
Where death and war consume all life.
The swords still clash, the arrows fly,
Yet I endure beneath the sky.
I seek the revered, the wise, the just,
To cleanse the world of blood and dust.
Yet where he dwells, I cannot say,
His visage veiled, his path astray.
The whispers of the slain surround,
Their voices weave a mournful sound.
They beg me, "Sing of us, O bard,
For we are gone, our tales are marred."
The sky above, a muted gray,
Shrouds the horrors of the day.
The sun hides low, ashamed to see
The chaos wrought by cruelty.
Through twisted trees and shattered land,
I clutch my lute with trembling hand.
Its strings, though frayed, still hum with grace,

A fleeting solace in this place.
For every note, a story told,
Of valour bright, of hearts grown cold.
The world must know the cost of war,
Of dreams destroyed, of peace no more.
I tread where shadows intertwine,
With specters grim, yet they are mine.
Each ghostly face, each mournful cry,
A fragment of the bard's own eye.
Oh fate, unkind, why must I bear
The weight of pain beyond compare?
Yet still I walk, yet still I sing,
For truth is life's eternal spring.
The winds may howl, the stars may fade,
But songs endure, though hearts are weighed.
And I, the bard, will weave my tune,
Beneath the sun, beneath the moon.
What talisman will shield me now,
As darkness drapes its solemn shroud?
What omen lights my weary path,
Through bloodied fields and nature's wrath?
Though I have lived a life so long,
My soul still yearns for one last song.
To sing of peace, to banish strife,
To honor those who gave their life.
Oh battlefield, your tale is grim,
Yet hope still lingers, faint and dim.
For even here, where sorrow's sown,
The seeds of love can yet be grown.

And as I tread this hallowed ground,
Where life and death are tightly bound,
I vow to seek the hidden den,
Where wisdom dwells beyond all men.
For in this quest, I'll find my peace,
A bard's resolve will never cease.
Through pain, through war, through death's embrace,
The song remains, a timeless grace.
So let the angels watch my plight,
As shadows turn to fading light.
For I will sing till breath is gone,
A bard eternal, traveling on.

25. The Devil's Bargain

Hail, O King of Jarbi, why dost thou quiver?
Do shadows haunt thee by the moonlit river?
Come hither, thou spirit bound by dread,
I rise to speak, though the righteous fled.
Encased in fear, thou dost falter still,
Yet power awaits thee, bent to thy will.
Adorned I stand in robes of despair,
A crown of darkness upon my hair.
Thy anger burns like a fire untamed,
Thy hunger grows for the glory unnamed.
Too far thou hast trudged, thy steps undone,
Yet closer I beckon, the pact begun.
Take now the gift that mortals desire,
Dominion unchallenged, kingdoms entire.
The night is thick with a shroud of dread,
No stars to guide thee, no prayers are said.
The trees stand bare, their whispers lost,
While Heaven's gates are frozen in frost.
But Hades yawns, its maw agape,
Awaiting those who choose their fate.
Why linger, King, in trembling fear?
The path to might is ever near.
Thy dreams of conquest, thy lust for fame,
All can be thine—if thou playest the game.

No armies nor blades can match my power,
No mortal force can break this hour.
I offer thee strength, unyielding might,
To vanquish foes, to claim the night.
But lo, the price thou must endure,
A single payment, steadfast and sure.
Thy soul, O King, thy essence divine,
Shall now and forevermore be mine.
The winds howl fierce as the pact draws near,
Thy silence speaks louder than cries of fear.
The earth shall tremble beneath thy reign,
Yet chains unseen shall bind thy name.
For glory sought on a cursed decree,
Will lead thy realm to misery.
The stars may fall, the skies may weep,
But the abyss shall claim what thou dost keep.
Do not delay, the hour is late,
Seal thy pact and embrace thy fate.
Power awaits thee, King of Jarbi,
Ruler eternal, yet never free.
For what is a throne, if shadows cling?
What worth is a crown if devils sing?
Once forged, this bond none can sever,
Thy soul shall wander my realm forever.
So choose, O King, with trembling hand,
The future thine, the night unmanned.
Repent, and the world shall turn away,
But regret thou canst not, come the day.

Stand tall, O King, make thy decree,
Shall Jarbi rise, or shall thou flee?
The Devil waits, with a grin so wide,
For the choice thou mak'st will turn the tide.
As the moon wanes and the shadows grow,
Decide, O King, to stay or go.
The Devil's bargain lies before thee,
Take it now, or forever flee.
But mark my words, if thou consent,
Eternal torment shall be thy lament.
For power gained through sin's embrace,
Shall leave thy kingdom a cursed place.
Hail, O King of Jarbi, the choice is thine,
To rule the earth, or let stars align.
The Devil's offer, sharp and clear,
Whispered low for thy soul to hear.
The winds shall howl, the earth shall quake,
What path thou choose, the dawn shall make.
So tremble not, and step forth true,
The Devil's bargain awaits for you.

26. The Sorcerer's Reign

The Horsemen of Condo, high they stand,
Their shadows etched on the mountain's hand.
Yet watch as they will, their gaze is weak,
For I am the storm, the vengeance they seek.
Their swords may gleam, their banners fly,
But they know not the truth of the sorcerer's sky.
No day of triumph hath crowned their quest,
While I wielded power in my perfect sweep, blessed.
Old and tattered, their spirits mourn,
Their lost souls adrift, broken, and worn.
No mortal desire, no lingering plea,
Can guide their steps to conquering me.
They claimed themselves heirs of battle and throne,
But I am the king, born of fire and stone.
My crown is forged in the furnace of might,
My dominion spans the endless night.
Behold my eyes, twin sapphires aglow,
Desires untamed in their sapphire flow.
No wound can harm me, no blade can bind,
For I am the master of space and time.
The ancient brine, from Kardos' rest,
Baptized my scars in its ocean's crest.
A blend of power, potent and rare,
Seeps through my veins like a storm in the air.

Oh, how I wish to rewind the clock,
To days when fate was a sealed lock.
To when these soldiers, valiant and proud,
Lay still in the womb, soft and unbowed.
For what are they now but pawns in my game,
Marching to meet their ruin and shame?
Their mortal frames, bound by the years,
Face an eternal master who has no fears.
I summon the winds, the sands, the tides,
Through time's corridors, my spirit glides.
While they wield steel and brute resolve,
My power bends what they cannot solve.
Shall I unmake them, strand by strand?
Erase their lineage with a wave of my hand?
Or let them linger, lost in despair,
As shadows haunt them through poisoned air?
The shores of Kardos call my name,
Where power eternal stoked my flame.
While they tremble, bound by the now,
I reign supreme with a timeless vow.
They march, unknowing, to their doom,
Fools caught in destiny's loom.
For I am not a sorcerer they can cage,
But a being unbound by mortal rage.
So come, O horsemen, face my might,
Challenge the fire, the ancient night.
Your fate is sealed, your end is clear,
For time itself bows when I appear.

I'll send you back to the womb's embrace,
To a time before your mortal trace.
Eras shall vanish, your names undone,
For I am the sorcerer, second to none.
From Kardos' rest to the mountains high,
The stars bear witness, the heavens sigh.
No sword can pierce, no spell can bind,
For I am the master of all mankind.
Now turn away, or face the cost,
Your hopes extinguished, your futures lost.
The Horsemen of Condo, high they stand,
But the sorcerer reigns over sea and land.

27. The Hermit's Embrace

O stranger who treads from Balore's decay,
Why climb the stairs of despair this day?
Thy silence whispers through wrathful halls,
A ghostly echo that softly calls.
Art thou the tormented, hooded and veiled,
A shadow of sorrow where light has failed?
Wandering far in a guise of despair,
Seeking a haven beyond the cold air?
Or art thou a weaver of time's silver thread,
A storyteller with tales of the dead?
Unveil thyself, shed sorrow's guise,
And let the warmth of my hearth arise.
Come forth, O soul, to the light of my fire,
Let its embrace soothe thy heart's desire.
Remove thy hood, let laughter ignite,
To banish the shadows of eternal night.
Tell me thy tale, thy woe and strife,
The trials endured through the scourge of life.
Let thy words entwine with the starry fangs,
As the night absorbs their mournful pangs.
The sky may break, its wounds may bleed,
Yet solace blooms where love plants its seed.
Come bathe in joy, a plundered delight,
Harvested from tales spun through the night.

The sea of stories churns with mirth,
Rising to banish the weight of the earth.
Pellets of laughter, though hollow they seem,
Can heal the soul and renew the dream.
Drink of my kindness, forget thy despair,
In this hermit's abode, thou art laid bare.
No curse shall linger, no scorn remain,
For here love thrives, absolving pain.
Thy scars are thy armor, thy pain thy lore,
A history carved in the depths of thy core.
Yet here thou art welcome, thy past forgone,
For the dawn shall rise, and the night be gone.
Thy hands may tremble, thy voice may wane,
But the warmth of this hearth shall dull thy pain.
Through the flicker of flames, thy soul shall mend,
In this sacred refuge where sorrows end.
No more an outcast, no more a shade,
The balm of compassion shall not fade.
For the bonds of humanity, fragile yet strong,
Can turn the mournful into a song.
O stranger of Balore, thou art not alone,
This hermit's heart is thy newfound throne.
Rest thy spirit, find solace here,
Let love prevail, and dissolve thy fear.
For the fangs of the night shall cease to bite,
When laughter and warmth fill the hollowed night.
Together we'll weave a tapestry bright,
Of hope reborn, and a soul's pure light.

So linger not, let thy burdens fall,
And answer the warmth of this humble call.
The ruins of Balore shall fade away,
As the promise of love heralds a new day.

28. The Song Within

If you wish to sing, then let it be so,

Do not hide where your true self won't show.

For yours is a voice, unique, divine,

A melody rare, a perfect design.

No other can match the tone you bear,

A voice so pure, beyond compare.

So sing for the moments that have slipped away,

For the dreams left silent and the words unsaid today.

Let your song rise like the break of dawn,

Through the mist of doubt where fears are drawn.

For life is fleeting, a river untamed,

A stage awaiting your song unclaimed.

Who knows when a soul will come near,

Drawn by your tune, their heart sincere?

To say, "Is this the voice I've sought?

The one whose song my spirit has caught?"

Do not let the silence be your refrain,

Break through the walls of fear and disdain.

The world may feel like a shadowed place,

But your song can cast a radiant grace.

Each note you sing is a story untold,

A fragment of courage, defiant and bold.

So lift your voice and cast aside,

The chains of doubt where shadows abide.

You are the enchanted, the perfect one,
Whose melody brightens like a rising sun.
A beacon of hope in the dim unknown,
A voice that transforms the cold into home.
Sing for yourself, for the joy it brings,
For the freedom found when the heartstrings sing.
Sing for the lonely, the quiet, the lost,
For the ones too afraid to bear the cost.
Let your song echo through valleys and skies,
Through moments of doubt and whispered goodbyes.
Sing for the stars that silently glow,
For they too shine though the world may not know.
The tune you carry, no one can repeat,
It's a rhythm of life, a pulse, a beat.
Each word, each note, a bridge you create,
To connect with the world and rewrite your fate.
So cast aside fear, let courage ignite,
Sing through the day, and into the night.
For the soul of the shy and the hearts subdued,
Will find their strength in your interlude.
When the day comes and you're heard at last,
The weight of silence will be the past.
And someone will say, with awe so true,
"Your song has drawn me closer to you."
For every voice has its place to belong,
And every heart hides a beautiful song.
Let yours be the one to inspire and heal,
To awaken the world, to make it feel.

So sing, O dreamer, let your courage grow,
Unveil your heart, let your music flow.
For life is a canvas, and your voice the hue,
Paint it with courage, bold and true.

29. The Stage of You

Don't be a mere spectator in this vast array,
A world of chaos, mirth, and dismay.
Stand tall, step forward, take your place,
For life's a stage you alone must grace.
Why blend into shadows, unseen, unheard,
When your voice could echo, your soul be stirred?
Why mimic the masks that others wear,
When your own truth is beyond compare?
Be the actor, not just the crowd,
Speak your lines clear, bold, and proud.
Whether the role is king or pauper,
Play it true, with courage proper.
The world will tempt, with shining lies,
To chase the trends, to seek disguise.
But no borrowed light can make you shine,
Only your own can truly align.
Each part you play, each word, each deed,
Fills the script of your soul's deep need.
Night and day, as the scenes unfold,
Write your story, unique and bold.
The costumes may fade, the roles may shift,
But your essence remains, your timeless gift.
No need to copy, to fake, to bend,
The truth you carry will transcend.

Dare to dream, to carve your way,
To break the molds of yesterday.
Let others follow their chosen path,
While you forge your own through life's aftermath.
The world's a mirror, reflecting all,
But your reflection must never fall.
Let it gleam with your distinct hue,
A masterpiece painted by only you.
For those who copy, who try to fit,
Lose themselves in a shallow script.
But those who embrace their spirit's call,
Find their freedom beyond the wall.
So play your part, and play it well,
From mountain peak to shadowed dell.
Be it joy, or grief, or trials severe,
Your authentic self will persevere.
When the final act comes into view,
And the curtains close on all you do,
It's not the applause or the fleeting fame,
But the truth you lived that earns acclaim.
So rise, dear soul, let your journey start,
With your voice, your mind, your beating heart.
Don't fade into echoes of someone else's view—
Take the stage, for the world needs you.

30. A Morning's Journey

Before the dawn begins to break,
When stars still shimmer, dreams awake,
I lie in quiet, soft repose,
Yet feel the call as morning grows.
A sigh escapes, the bed feels warm,
But habit nudges, sets the norm.
With heavy limbs, I push, I rise,
Chasing whispers of the skies.
No screen distracts my waking eyes,
No flood of news, no buzzing lies.
Instead, the day begins with care,
A sacred rhythm, pure and rare.
A splash of water, crisp and cool,
A cleansing wave, a morning rule.
Chores hum softly in the air,
A melody of love and prayer.
A simple sip, a glass of life,
Quenching dreams, dispelling strife.
And then the woods, my feet take flight,
Toward realms of green and morning light.
The world awaits, serene, untamed,
A timeless canvas, wild, unnamed.
Beneath the boughs of towering trees,
I find a symphony in the breeze.

Each step a hymn, each breath a song,
The earth and I, where both belong.
Leaves dance gently, kissed by dew,
The sun ascends, a golden hue.
Birds awaken, their chorus pure,
A fleeting moment, yet so sure.
The rustle of the woodland floor,
A language ancient, hearts implore.
The path unfolds, a winding thread,
Where nature's wonders pull me ahead.
The streams that murmur, rocks that gleam,
All weave the fabric of a dream.
Through shaded glens and sunlit trails,
Through whispering winds and fragrant gales,
I jog with purpose, soul alight,
Each moment bursting with delight.
The forest heals, its quiet art,
Restores the spirit, mends the heart.
Its beauty speaks, a voice profound,
Of timeless truths in life unbound.
And as the morning stretches wide,
I hold its treasures deep inside.
The woods may end, the chores resume,
But in my soul, the flowers bloom.
For every dawn, a chance anew,
To chase the light, embrace the view.
To rise, to run, to breathe, to be,
Alive within this harmony.

31. The Measure of a Life

One day, when I am old and gray,
And life's long whispers fade away,
I'll leave behind my wealth, my gold,
The fortunes earned, the stories told.
The sweat of youth, the toil, the tears,
The hours spent across the years.
But can these treasures buy more time,
Another breath, a chance to climb?
Perhaps they'll stand in silent halls,
Or gather dust upon cold walls.
The coins I chased, the deals I made,
A fleeting echo, soon to fade.
Will they recall the sums I earned,
Or the moments when my kindness burned?
Will they count the riches in my chest,
Or how I gave my heart its best?
For time is cruel, it marches fast,
And every breath becomes the past.
The clock won't pause for wealth or fame,
It plays for all a constant game.
If heaven calls or hell awaits,
I'll meet my fate beyond the gates.
But in that moment, standing still,
I'll weigh the void I tried to fill.

Did I laugh, did I love, did I truly live?
Did I learn to take, did I learn to give?
Or did I trade my dreams away,
For fleeting things that rot and decay?
So hear me now, you fleeting souls,
With lists to check and endless goals:
Pause a moment, breathe, be free,
And carve your name in memory.
For when the curtain starts to fall,
It's love and joy that we'll recall.
Not gold, not lands, not lofty towers,
But the seeds we sow in quiet hours.
Spend your time in ways that shine,
With laughter sweet and love divine.
The wealth you build, the legacy—
Let it be life, in all its beauty.

32. The Infinite Within

When shadows fall and silence sings,
And loneliness sharpens its bitter stings,
When the crowd feels hollow, faces unknown,
And you stand, lost, as if alone—
Pause a moment, and gaze beyond,
Through the window, where rain responds,
Each drop, a story, a fleeting trace,
Disappearing swiftly, yet leaving grace.
The rain that falls, so brief its flight,
Fulfills a purpose in the grander light.
It quenches the earth, it feeds the streams,
It nourishes life, fulfills unseen dreams.
Look to the sun, its beams that glow,
Traveling light-years to let you know—
Each ray, a purpose, though unseen,
It lights the world and all in between.
Feel the wind as it dances through,
Tossing your hair in a wild ado.
Though invisible, it stirs the air,
A whisper of purpose, beyond compare.
So why, dear soul, do you despair?
Why let rejection dim your flare?
Your worth's not proven by worldly eyes,
Your essence blends with the infinite skies.

The stars above, the earth below,
Each has a purpose, a truth to show.
The smallest grain, the tallest tree,
All are threads in infinity.
You're more than your fears, your wounds, your pain,
You're the gentle sunbeam, the soothing rain.
Not here to battle, to prove, or to fight,
But to blend with the cosmos and share your light.
Know this truth and hold it tight:
You're never alone in the endless night.
You are the wind, the rain, the sun,
A piece of the whole, a part of the One.
Your steps may falter, your voice may break,
Yet each move forward, the stars awake.
A purpose lies, though hidden and veiled,
A voyage to sail, a dream to be hailed.
So lift your heart and find your flame,
You're not a shadow, you're not to blame.
You are the infinite, vast and free,
A symphony sung in eternity.
And when you blend, release, and flow,
You'll find the truth: you've always known.
That lost, rejected, lonely you seem,
You're part of a universal dream.
No longer bound, no longer confined,
You are the cosmos, perfectly aligned.
And in that blending, you will see,
You were never lost—just meant to be.

33. The Unheard Song

Some songs are never sung aloud,
Yet linger softly, unseen but proud.
In the silence, their whispers stay,
Guiding hearts that have lost their way.
They float on winds, on dreams untold,
In shadows where the weary fold.
A hymn for those who ache and yearn,
A tune of hope for hearts to discern.
When the storm roars wild and fierce,
And life feels like a wound to pierce,
These songs emerge, serene and low,
A quiet warmth in a world of snow.
Not every voice must rise and shout;
Some melodies live in hearts devout.
They wait in patience, in twilight's hue,
For someone longing to listen anew.
The heavy heart, weighed by despair,
Finds solace in the songs that care.
Unseen by the eyes, unfelt by the hand,
Yet they comfort, like waves on the sand.
When thunder crashes and lightning flares,
And the soul is burdened by endless cares,
These songs become the gentle rain,
Washing away the fear and pain.

A listener waits, through storm and gale,
Hoping for whispers that never fail.
In longing's arms, his heart does rest,
For he knows these songs are love's behest.
Some melodies bloom in the still of night,
A spark of hope, a fleeting light.
They hum through tears, through grief's embrace,
A silent strength, a healing grace.
The gentle rain begins to fall,
Answering the unheard call.
Its drops are notes, its rhythm pure,
A hymn of solace, steady and sure.
When life feels barren, dark, and stark,
And shadows linger, deep and stark,
These songs will hum, though faint they be,
A timeless hymn of eternity.
So hear them now, with heart unbound,
The songs in silence, profound, profound.
They speak of courage, of love untamed,
Of hope rekindled, of fears reclaimed.
For every soul who longs to heal,
These unheard songs, their truths reveal.
They lift the weary, the lost, the broken,
A balm of peace in words unspoken.
So when the storm has raged and gone,
And life feels fragile, a fleeting dawn,
Listen closely, the song remains—
A whispered joy through gentle rains.

These songs unseen, they're always near,
A steady hand when life feels unclear.
Unheard, unsung, yet ever there,
For those who seek, for those who care.
Let them guide you, soft and true,
Through storms that pass, through skies of blue.
And when you rise, your heart grown strong,
You'll know you were saved by an unheard song.

34. The Melody of Life

If you unwind the clock, let its hands run free,
You'll hear its tick, a steady decree.
The rhythm of time, its quiet refrain,
A song of moments, joy and pain.
Stop for a while, just pause your stride,
Let the world's music be your guide.
The birds go chirp, a melody pure,
The bees hum softly, their tune secure.
Life hums a song, so rich and deep,
Yet you rush past, its secrets keep.
The symphony calls with gentle grace,
A treasure unseen in life's fast race.
The rustle of leaves, the whispering trees,
The playful dance of a summer breeze.
Each sound a note, a tale it tells,
From ocean waves to chiming bells.
The patter of rain, a calming tune,
A serenade sung beneath the moon.
The laughter of children, a joyous sound,
Echoes of love the world around.
Yet we rush, we run, our hearts confined,
Blind to the wonders we leave behind.
Caught in the race for dreams untold,
We miss life's treasures, worth more than gold.

Lose a little hope, just for today,
Set it aside, let wonder play.
Not to despair, but to embrace,
The magic of moments, life's warm embrace.
For hope can blind, can steal your view,
Of the present joys life offers you.
It chains the heart to future schemes,
While life unfolds in golden streams.
Pause for the tick, the tock, the hum,
For the gentle beats of a distant drum.
Let go of haste, let time unfold,
Its melody rich, its stories bold.
The breeze that lifts, the sun's soft kiss,
These fleeting gifts you must not miss.
The world is alive, a grand ballet,
Inviting you to dance today.
The solo of silence, the chorus of sound,
The echoes of wonder all around.
Each note, each chord, a tale divine,
A song of life, your life, and mine.
So pause the clock, let stillness reign,
Hear life's music soothe your pain.
No need to chase, to win, to gain,
The gift of now is worth the refrain.
And when you stop to hear and see,
The melody flows, wild and free.
A tune of joy, of grace, of care,
A timeless song that's always there.

Don't let it pass, don't let it fade,
This symphony life so gently made.
For when you listen, you'll finally know,
The beauty in life's tick-tack-tow.

35. The Phoenix Within

When death spits hard, cold in your face,
And life deserts you, leaves no trace,
Yet deep inside, a spark ignites,
A flame reborn from shadowed nights.
Like a phoenix rising, born of fire,
From ashes wrought, your heart aspires.
You feel the pulse, the surge, the cry,
Alive again, you pierce the sky.
In shadows deep, where hope seems frail,
You find your strength, you lift the veil.
Beneath neon lights that burn so bright,
You claim the dark and seize the night.
Defying fear, you take your flight,
Soaring high through endless night.
Each wing a whisper, each beat a roar,
Unleashing a power you'd lost before.
On the edge of sight, where danger lies,
You face the storm, defy the skies.
A killer thrill, a daring chase,
You conquer the blood curdling space.
Each fall you take, each wound you bear,
Builds the strength you've learned to wear.
The scars you carry, your badge of pride,
Proof you've lived, you've thrived, you've tried.

Through broken dreams and shattered days,
You've forged your fire, you've lit the blaze.
The shadows watch, but cannot consume,
The light you wield, the life you resume.
You rise again, though torn apart,
With grit in soul and steel in heart.
No force can bind, no fear can tether,
A phoenix soul is born forever.
Through the neon glow, through chaos and haze,
You stride with purpose, your spirit ablaze.
Each step you take, a rebel's song,
In the face of defeat, you prove them wrong.
Life may falter, its colours fade,
But you rebuild, unafraid.
In killer spaces, you stake your claim,
Each pulse, each breath, a fearless flame.
You soar where others fear to tread,
Defying odds, defying dread.
The dark may call, the shadows cling,
But you are the phoenix, born to sing.
So live on the edge, where courage gleams,
In the world of fire and vivid dreams.
Let the darkness quake, let the shadows shiver,
For your blazing soul will burn forever.
No chains can hold, no fate confine,
The power within, the spark divine.
A phoenix rises, unbroken, free,
A living testament to eternity.

36. The Leap of Dreams

Every beautiful dream, a shining light,
Can turn to shadow, shrouded in night.
If fear takes hold, its grip so tight,
The dream fades away, out of sight.
For those afraid to lose or fall,
Will never scale the highest wall.
The unknown whispers, calling you near,
To face your doubts, to shed your fear.
Jump into the void, let courage soar,
Beyond the safe, there's always more.
The world unfolds where bold hearts tread,
A canvas waiting, where dreams are fed.
To step into the great unknown,
Is to plant a seed where hope is sown.
Each risk a path, a truth to find,
An uncharted journey for heart and mind.
For life is more than cautious days,
It's daring leaps, untrodden ways.
To stay behind is to remain the same,
But a leap can spark a brighter flame.
Dreams unleashed, like wings unbound,
Take flight where endless skies surround.
The wind may howl, the storm may roar,
But brave hearts always seek the more.

A choice may seem the safer call,
Yet a leap can conquer the fear of fall.
The treasures lie where risks are taken,
Where souls are stirred, and hearts awaken.
The unknown may seem a daunting place,
But it holds the thrill of a boundless space.
For in each step where courage burns,
A piece of wisdom, the dreamer earns.
What if you fail? What if you break?
What if it's all a grand mistake?
But what if you soar, what if you thrive?
What if your leap keeps dreams alive?
To leap is to trust in your inner fire,
To chase the path of your soul's desire.
And though the journey may test your will,
The climb is worth the daunting hill.
Each step of faith, each daring dive,
Keeps the spark of wonder alive.
For only by leaping can you uncover,
A world unseen, a truth to discover.
So take the risk, don't shy away,
Let fear dissolve with the break of day.
The unknown beckons, its promise true,
A risk worth taking, a dream anew.
Don't let the beauty of dreams decay,
By fear of loss, or doubt's dismay.
Leap into life, embrace its streams,
For only then will you live your dreams.

37. Write the Story of You

The best stories wait, unwritten, untold,
A treasure within, more precious than gold.
The ink of your life, so vivid, so true,
The pages are blank, the author is you.
When will you start? The moment is now,
To take up the pen, to make your vow.
A bestseller waits in your heart's embrace,
A tale of triumph, of courage, of grace.
Let the world see your biography clear,
A story of hope that others hold dear.
For within your struggles, your rise, your fall,
Lies a spark of light to inspire us all.
Write of the dreams you dared to chase,
The fears you faced, the trials you embraced.
Of the paths untraveled, the risks you took,
The lessons you learned from each page and nook.
No need for grandeur, no need for fame,
Each chapter of life is a worthy acclaim.
Your story's yours, unique, profound,
A legacy written where truth is found.
The world awaits your open book,
To read your soul with every look.
For each life lived has wisdom to give,
A map for others to learn and live.

Don't wait for tomorrow, don't hesitate,
This moment now is your perfect state.
Pick up the pen, let your spirit flow,
Through words and lines, let your essence glow.
Write of the laughter, the tears, the fight,
The moments of shadow, the bursts of light.
Write of the times you stood your ground,
When courage within you was finally found.
For each story shared, a light is lit,
In hearts that seek the courage to fit.
Your tale can heal, can guide, can teach,
A legacy lasting, its power will reach.
The bestseller of life is not in the sale,
But in the hearts where your truths prevail.
Let the world turn your pages with awe,
And marvel at the life you once saw.
So be the author of your days ahead,
Write with passion, with purpose, unsaid.
Let each chapter be filled with the fire,
Of dreams fulfilled, of souls inspired.
For the best stories are not about fame,
But the spark within, a glowing flame.
So tell the world, your story's begun,
A tale of a life where greatness was won.
Write now, don't wait for the years to fade,
For the book of your life is yet to be made.
Be the bestseller of your own design,
A beacon of hope, a star that will shine.

38. In the Mirror of Time

Live in the moments, not in the years,
For time is a stream that silently clears.
The future is hidden, a tale untold,
The past is a shadow, a memory cold.
Do not chase sunsets already gone,
Nor pine for stars that haven't yet shone.
The now is a treasure, gleaming and bright,
A fleeting flame in the depth of the night.
As long as your breath fills the open air,
Be bold, be joyful, be free from despair.
Laugh with abandon, dance in the rain,
Let your heart sing its sweetest refrain.
Fall in love and take the chance,
Be it a fleeting or timeless romance.
Quarrel, forgive, and embrace anew,
Life is a song with ever-changing hue.
Do not wait for the perfect day,
For time and tide will not delay.
The clock's hands turn, they never pause,
Celebrate life without a cause.
Admire yourself for all you are,
A luminous soul, your own guiding star.
Look in the mirror, see what is true,
The person reflected is beautifully you.

Love your body, a vessel divine,
A masterpiece crafted in cosmic design.
Cherish each wrinkle, each scar, each line,
They tell your story, they make you shine.
Do not let doubts or fears intrude,
Banish the voices that try to exclude.
The world outside may be cruel or kind,
But your worth is something they cannot define.
Hold your head high, face the skies,
Even when clouds dim your sunrise.
For every storm shall pass away,
Revealing the dawn of a brighter day.
Dream, but do not let dreams confine,
For life is here, in this very line.
Do not trade your today for a tomorrow,
Nor sink your heart in yesterday's sorrow.
Take the risks that your soul desires,
Let passion burn like eternal fires.
Let failures teach, let triumphs inspire,
And keep reaching higher and higher.
You are the artist, the brush, the hue,
The canvas of life depends on you.
Paint it boldly, with colours wild,
Be curious, daring, and endlessly styled.
Do not compare your light to another,
Each star has a glow like no other.
Shine in your way, embrace your grace,
And leave your mark in time's vast space.

So live in moments, savor them all,
The rise of the sun, the night's gentle call.
Celebrate small joys, a smile, a breeze,
The rustle of leaves, the whispers of trees.
Life is a gift, a fleeting embrace,
A journey through time, a wondrous race.
Do not count days or measure in years,
Live boldly, love fully, and silence your fears.
For in the mirror, the truth resides,
A soul unbroken, a heart that abides.
Admire the person who meets your gaze,
Their light is eternal, their beauty ablaze.
So take this moment, hold it tight,
Make it your beacon, your guiding light.
For the past is gone, and the future unclear,
But today is yours—live it sincere.

39. The Road of Thorns

Do not halt when shadows press near,

When failure whispers in your ear.

The path may seem a bitter fight,

But even darkness yields to light.

You've stumbled, fallen, lost your way,

But every night turns into day.

Life is not a race to win,

Nor a tally of loss or sin.

It's rising up when the odds defy,

Spreading your wings and learning to fly.

For every fall is a lesson learned,

Each scar a badge, a triumph earned.

Hope may seem like a distant star,

Faint and flickering, faintly afar.

But stars are guides in the darkest skies,

They light the path for steadfast eyes.

Don't count defeats, don't curse the rain,

Each drop will cleanse, not deepen the pain.

The road of thorns may pierce and sting,

Yet through it all, your spirit will sing.

For roses bloom beyond the strife,

Their beauty carved by trials of life.

The sweetest fruits, the brightest flame,

Are born from struggles, forged by flame.

Failures teach what victories can't,
The power of dreams, the strength to plant.
Seeds of courage in fields of despair,
To bloom where others would not dare.
The journey ahead is yours to tread,
With fearless heart and lifted head.
Each step you take, though slow, unsure,
Builds a future strong and pure.
When thorns tear flesh and doubts invade,
Recall the progress your courage made.
For even the tallest mountains bow,
To those who climb with sweat on their brow.
Life is a climb, a winding road,
A heavy, yet glorious, shifting load.
You may not always reach the peak,
But every stride makes you unique.
The world will test, it always does,
With trials, heartbreak, and a lingering "because."
But beyond the storm, the sun will rise,
Clearing the tears from your weary eyes.
Don't fear to fall; embrace the ground,
For strength in failure is often found.
Each stumble shapes, each bruise refines,
Transforming you through life's designs.
You'll walk through fire, you'll face the gale,
Yet through it all, your soul won't pale.
The road of thorns may make you bleed,
But it will grant the strength you need.

For every thorn that pricks your skin,
A future blossom grows within.
The flowers bloom for those who strive,
Who rise again, who stay alive.
So walk with purpose, unbowed, unbroken,
Let hope be your shield, your unspoken token.
The world is yours, the path is wide,
And beauty waits on the other side.
Remember, life is not a score,
It's a journey to discover more.
More strength, more grace, more love, more light,
A dance through shadow, a climb to height.
Do not let failure dim your fire,
Let it be fuel for dreams to aspire.
For victory is not in the prize,
But in the strength to once again rise.
So tread the thorns with steady heart,
Embrace the challenge, play your part.
And when you've walked through trials dire,
You'll stand among the blooms you admire.
Let each thorn remind, each bruise recall,
You walked through it, you conquered it all.
For beyond the pain, the toil, the strife,
Lies the garden of a meaningful life.

40. The Last Sunset

One day, the sun will bow to the sea,
Its light dimming softly, embracing me.
The horizon painted in scarlet and gold,
Like a bride adorned, her beauty untold.
The dusk will come with its tender kiss,
A fleeting warmth, a moment of bliss.
It will touch my lips, a gentle embrace,
As shadows gather, veiling the space.
I'll stand alone, watching far and wide,
The vast expanse where dreams collide.
The whispers of time, so faint, so clear,
Will remind me my end is near.
But even as my days grow few,
My heart will cling to what is true.
The fire within will refuse to die,
Even as stars claim the fading sky.
The sleepless night will welcome me,
A silent vigil by eternity's tree.
The weight of time, the breath of years,
Will dissolve in the stream of forgotten tears.
I'll lie down calm, yet fiercely alive,
For the essence of life will always strive.
The body may falter, the spirit may fade,
But the will to endure will never be swayed.

Each heartbeat, a song, a defiant tune,
A dance beneath the silver moon.
Each breath, a vow to the skies above,
A testament of hope, a hymn of love.
When the stars appear, so cold, so bright,
They will mirror my soul, my inner light.
For though my body rests in the earth,
My spirit shall rise to prove its worth.
I will not fear the eternal sleep,
For life is a promise we're meant to keep.
To hold on tight to the last fleeting thread,
Even as the cosmos calls me to bed.
The wind will whisper through the trees,
Carrying my essence across the seas.
The earth will cradle my weary frame,
Yet my spirit will burn, an eternal flame.
I'll linger in sunsets, in morning dew,
In the laughter of children, the skies so blue.
The world will carry my presence still,
In the rustle of leaves, the strength of a hill.
Even if I am gone from sight,
My essence will linger, a guiding light.
In every heart that dares to dream,
I'll flow like water in life's endless stream.
The horizon is not an end to me,
But a doorway to infinity.
A journey beyond, a path untold,
Through mysteries vast, and stars of gold.

And as the sun sets for the final time,
I'll rise in verses, in stories, in rhyme.
For though I may vanish, I'll never depart,
I'll live forever in each beating heart.
So when the dusk comes dressed in red,
And whispers softly, "Rest your head,"
Know that the spark within remains,
An ember that no force contains.
One day, the sun will set for me,
But my will to linger will always be.
To touch the world, to leave a trace,
A love eternal in time's embrace.

41. The Time You Never Know

When the time to go, you never know,

Like a fleeting breeze or the river's flow.

O hapless man, why waste the days,

Chasing shadows in life's endless maze?

Fall in love, if only for a while,

Let your heart be warmed by a tender smile.

Hold a hand, feel the world anew,

Let moments of joy embrace you, too.

Why climb mountains too steep to scale,

Or chase the winds with dreams so frail?

Forget the wealth, the crown, the fame,

They're fleeting fires that play no game.

Life is a whisper, a fleeting spark,

A flame that flickers against the dark.

So rest awhile in your lover's arms,

And bask in the glow of their quiet charms.

For what are riches compared to this?

The simple magic of a stolen kiss.

The world can wait, its golden throne,

For love's sweet touch is wealth alone.

Forget the high ambitions you hold,

The castles of silver, the mountains of gold.

They pale before the light in her eyes,
A universe within where true beauty lies.
The ticking clock has a silent stride,
And time won't wait, nor run nor hide.
It slips like sand through open hands,
A fleeting tale no one understands.
So laugh today, while you still can,
Dance in the rain, O hapless man.
Embrace the fleeting, the here, the now,
Don't wait for life to show you how.
For tomorrow's dawn may never break,
And love left unspoken is life's mistake.
The arms you cherish may soon grow cold,
A story left unfinished, untold.
Do not let pride or dreams too high
Keep you from watching the stars in the sky.
Do not let riches chain your soul,
For love is the only true treasure to hold.
Who knows when time will call your name,
A quiet end to life's burning flame?
Who knows when you'll stand alone,
A heart left empty, a love overthrown?
So while you have breath and love to give,
Take this fleeting moment and truly live.
Let the world turn with its endless din,
For love is the battle you're meant to win.
Forget the clocks, their endless chime,
They cannot measure love or time.
Forget the road that stretches far,

Stay in the moment, where blessings are.
For the sun may rise, yet clouds may hide,
And fate may shift with the ocean tide.
One moment you're here, the next you're gone,
A fleeting note in life's endless song.
So rest, my friend, in her embrace,
Trace the lines of her cherished face.
Let her laughter be your sweetest tune,
A melody sung beneath the moon.
The world can wait, its urgent calls,
Its towering peaks, its gilded halls.
For nothing compares to love's warm glow,
A gift unmeasured by all we know.
When the time to go, you never see,
It comes like the wind on a restless sea.
But while you're here, let your heart stay true,
And love for a moment, or maybe a few.
Hold her close as the stars ignite,
A brief, eternal, celestial night.
For who can say when the time will part
Two souls entwined, one beating heart?
Live not for ambition, nor for gold,
But for the story your love will unfold.
For life is fleeting, a precious spark,
A blaze of light in the endless dark.
And when the end comes, as it must,
Let your heart be free of regret and dust.
For love, not riches, is what will remain,
A timeless echo, a sweet refrain.

So fall in love, let your spirit soar,
For in love's arms, you'll find what's more.
And when you're gone, the world will know,
You lived in moments that truly glow.

42. A Night in Hell's Delight

Through a veil of mist, I wandered late,
Seeking warmth, or perhaps my fate.
What lay ahead? A soothing glow?
Or just the devil's evening show?
I squeezed right through with a curious gait,
Wondering what horrors might await.
And there it was—a cauldron vast,
Bubbling with sins of ages past.
Sulfur and oil danced in the brew,
While agonized screams added a pleasant hue.
Men flailed about, women wailed,
In this fiery circus where all had failed.
Closer I crept, my heart agape,
Half from terror, half to escape.
But what did I see? A figure so lean,
Fragile limbs with a hooded sheen.
He staggered forth, or was it a prance?
Maybe Hell was teaching interpretive dance.
"Welcome to Hell!" he said with flair,
"We've got despair to spare—pull up a chair!"
"Meet your friends, embrace the pain,
Shake their hands—they've much to explain.
See the guy with the melting face?
He cheated taxes. Now he's disgraced."

"And that lady screaming in fiery loops?
She spread gossip—now she soups.
Hell's got a flair for poetic twists,
We punish sins you never knew exist!"
"Wait," I stammered, "I'm not sweating.
I'm calm, no groaning, no regretting."
He peered at me, his sockets hollow,
"Ah, your turn's not here, but it'll follow."
"Back you go, through the misty seam,
To live your life—or build more steam.
Change your trace or stay on course,
Your choices fuel this infernal force."
I retraced my steps, though part of me stayed,
Curious about the games Hell played.
But soon I woke, the morning stark,
The dream still vivid, twisted and dark.
Now here I sit, a lesson learned,
Yet somehow laughing at all I've discerned.
Life's a stage, and we're all the cast,
Slipping and sliding to the very last.
So why not dance, why not jest?
Make mistakes but do your best.
For in the end, Hell's hooded crew
Might just be waiting to welcome you.
Imagine the screams, the fiery stew,
But throw in jokes—they'll burn well too.
Shake hands with regret, or wave it goodbye,
It's all a comedy once you die.

So take your sins, your quirks, your flaws,
Don't fear the devil, his absurd applause.
Live your life with a chuckle, a wink,
For Hell's a riot if you stop to think.
And when your time comes, as surely it will,
To step through the veil and climb the hill,
May your laugh echo, your grin be wide—
After all, who wants a boring ride?

43. The Voice Within

There came a time in my darkest days,

When the world seemed cloaked in shadowy haze.

Rejection and sorrow like storms did swell,

My heart was a prisoner in a silent cell.

A torrent of thoughts, complaints untold,

Could fill the oceans with tales so cold.

Yet I chose not to voice my despair,

For in solitude, I found treasures rare.

In that quiet, a spark took hold,

An ember within, both fierce and bold.

Anger and pain, like a raging fire,

Could destroy a village or lift it higher.

The choice was mine—this I knew,

To let it consume or create anew.

So I listened close to the heart inside,

Where dreams and fears in whispers abide.

"Open your arms," the voice implored,

"And reach for the sky, let your spirit soar.

Or shrink in your shell, a safe retreat,

Where the ground feels steady beneath your feet."

I stood with courage and stretched my hand,

To grasp the clouds, soft as sand.

They slipped away, though thick they seemed,

A fleeting wisp, a distant dream.

Higher I climbed, to touch the stars,
To reach the heavens, to break the bars.
But as I ascended, I lost the feel,
Of earth beneath, so solid, so real.
The ground was gone, and fear took hold,
Ambition, once burning, now felt cold.
I let go of the grasp, the futile climb,
And fell back down, to a darker time.
Back to the place where dreams lay broken,
Where silence reigned, and no words were spoken.
Among the crowd, I stood forlorn,
Their laughter mocking, their faces worn.
They stayed where they were, safe and still,
While I had dared to climb the hill.
Yet here I was, lower than low,
Where ambition rots and failures grow.
I recoiled like the snail, retreating within,
Silencing the voice of the heart again.
But deep inside, a truth remained,
A lesson learned through loss and pain.
Failure is not the end, I found,
But a place to rise, to stand unbound.
For every fall teaches the soul to soar,
And opens the path to something more.
So I reached once more, with trembling hand,
Not for the stars or the promised land,
But for the courage to simply be,
To write my truth, to set it free.

The voice within, though crushed before,
Became my guide, my inner lore.
It whispered, "Fall if you must, but rise,
For every tear births clearer skies."
Now I walk with a steady stride,
No longer seeking the world to bide.
For the infinite lies not above,
But in the heart that dares to love.
And so, I write with the fire inside,
Turning pain to hope, fear to pride.
The voice within now sings with might,
In every word, I find my light.
To those who falter, hear me well,
The fall is where your courage will swell.
Open your arms, let your spirit fly,
For even in darkness, the stars still lie.

44. The Heart's Awakening

I felt ossified, frozen in place,
A relic of time in its endless race.
Not in my body, though it too grew still,
But in the heart that once dared to thrill.
Oscitant senses, dulled and numb,
Silent beats of a song unsung.
My veins, my sinews, no longer alive,
Struggling merely to survive.
Otiose, useless, I wandered through,
A world of glitter, but none of it true.
Shimmering lights and illusions vast,
Yet none could unshackle the chains of my past.
Confined, imprisoned, my spirit lay,
Within an oubliette where dreams decay.
My thoughts a labyrinth of shadows deep,
A restless mind where illusions creep.
But in that abyss, a whisper grew,
A faint yet steady voice breaking through.
"Why do you linger in this dismal space?
Why let the darkness obscure your grace?"
I paused to listen, my breath held tight,
For the voice was my own, a flickering light.
It spoke of dreams I had left to fade,
Of passions abandoned, hopes betrayed.

"You are not the stone you believe you are,
Within you burns a celestial star.
Break free from the walls that hold you fast,
Rise from the ruins of your weary past."
With trembling hands, I reached for the key,
To unlock the cage that encased me.
The weight of sorrow, heavy and old,
Fell from my shoulders, and courage took hold.
The world of glamour, once so bright,
Now seemed hollow in the new dawn's light.
For what is gold if it blinds the eye,
What are riches if they make you sigh?
I stepped beyond the veil of my mind,
To a world where purpose was yet to find.
Each step a triumph, each breath a song,
Each moment a chance to right the wrong.
The ossified heart began to beat,
Its rhythm steady, its cadence sweet.
Blood flowed through veins long thought dry,
As I reached for the limitless sky.
No longer otiose, no longer still,
I moved with purpose, driven by will.
For the oubliette that once held me tight,
Had vanished beneath the morning light.
Now I embrace both time and age,
Each line on my face a living page.
A story of triumph, of rising above,
A journey guided by hope and love.

So hear me, you who feel confined,
By the chains of fear within your mind.
You are not stone, you are not ash,
You are the spark that ignites the flash.
Break free from illusions, let shadows fall,
And answer the voice within your call.
For life awaits beyond despair,
A radiant path through the open air.
No longer ossified, I stand anew,
Alive with dreams that once withdrew.
The heart within beats strong and free,
And whispers, "This is who you're meant to be."

45. The Whispering Jungle

There's a jungle out there, dark and deep,
Where shadows stir while you softly sleep.
It calls your name through the midnight breeze,
A haunting hymn through the ancient trees.
"Leave your den," it murmurs low,
"Forsake the warmth where fires glow.
Abandon the sun, forget the day,
Step into the night, let fear hold sway."
The moon is a dagger, sharp and bright,
Cutting the silence, igniting the night.
Predators prowl with eyes agleam,
Drawing you closer, as if in a dream.
Run through the woods where shadows creep,
Where roots entwine and secrets seep.
The path is thorned, the ground is wild,
Each step untamed, each fear beguiled.
Climb the mountains, their jagged spires,
Lit by the blaze of spectral fires.
The air is thin, the wind a scream,
Each breath a tether to a fleeting dream.
Swim in torrents, the waters rage,
A liquid prison, a watery cage.
But still, you dive, the currents churn,
A siren's call you cannot spurn.

Run with the predators, sleek and fierce,
Through brambles sharp, through night that pierce.
Your pulse a drum, your heart a snare,
Entwined with the wild, a primal affair.
Become nocturnal, embrace the dark,
Let shadows carve their cryptic mark.
For light has no place in this eerie domain,
Only the whispers of joy and pain.
Live your greatest fear, let it rise,
Feel it writhe beneath starless skies.
Relive it again, until it's tamed,
Until your soul is unashamed.
The jungle breathes, alive, profound,
A realm of wonder and horrors unbound.
Its voice grows louder, its grip turns tight,
Pulling you further from morning's light.
Outshine the mundane, break the chain,
Of life's dull rhythm, its constant refrain.
For mediocrity is a deathly blight,
And the jungle offers a wilder fight.
Leap from the cliffs, defy the fall,
Answer the wild's unyielding call.
Let fear be your guide, let instinct steer,
For the unknown holds no room for tears.
Through tangled roots and torrents wide,
Through jagged peaks and endless tide,
Your spirit roars, no longer tame,
A creature reborn, without a name.

The jungle whispers, "You now belong,
To a life less ordinary, wild and strong."
And though the path may claim its toll,
You've traded comfort to find your soul.
So venture forth where shadows play,
Where dawn dissolves, and night holds sway.
For in the jungle, dark and grand,
Life is carved by your own hand.

46. Rich to the Bones

You may be rich to the bones, they say,
But how much hunger have you kept at bay?
Pockets lined with gold may shine,
Yet what of the empty plates you decline?
A million earned, a treasure vast,
But can it buy the time that's passed?
Time slips through fingers, fine as sand,
No wealth can grasp it, nor command.
You boast of riches, a kingly hoard,
Yet in your heart, no kindness stored.
Coins may jingle, jewels may gleam,
But can they weave a lasting dream?
When you are gone, your gold remains,
For others to squander, for others' gains.
No hymn of praise, no song will rise,
For selfish hearts earn no allies.
Like a hog fattened, its worth in death,
You'll leave behind no cherished breath.
The wealth you hoarded, the life you led,
A hollow echo, a path of dread.
If you wish to be rich, extend your deeds,
Sow goodwill's seeds, fulfill true needs.
For silver tongues and golden crowns,
Cannot replace a soul that drowns.

The weary and hungry, do they know your face?
Have you shared with them your life's embrace?
Or turned away with a heart of stone,
A monarch seated on a brittle throne?
A dime or a million, the tale's the same,
You'll eat a morsel, not feast in fame.
You'll wear a shirt, not a silken tent,
Life's bare essentials, where wealth is spent.
Riches grow stale, like bread left out,
What's wealth without love to tout?
A man with gold, but no one near,
Is a hollow king, his realm unclear.
Actions, not riches, will write your name,
In the hearts of others, your true acclaim.
For a feast unshared is a feast unblessed,
And a selfish soul finds no rest.
So lend your hand, and give your time,
Let kindness be your greatest climb.
For treasures lie in a gentle smile,
Not in vaults that stretch a mile.
They say money talks, but actions roar,
A wealth of goodwill opens more doors.
Feed the hungry, clothe the cold,
Share your riches, a heart of gold.
Extend your hands, not just your greed,
For life is judged by the deeds you seed.
A man remembered for love and care,
Is richer than kings beyond compare.

When you are gone, let them say with pride,
"Here lies one who stood by our side."
For in the end, it's not the gold you amassed,
But the kindness shared that will truly last.
So cast your bread upon the waves,
Give freely, even as the heart braves.
For though wealth may glitter and shine,
The true gem is a soul divine.

47. Beyond Measure

You stand in the market, priced at mere coins,
A treasure unmatched, yet bound in false joins.
Your worth is a jewel, an unyielding glow,
But the world, blindfolded, refuses to know.
They measure your value with scales untrue,
Their narrow minds cloud what shines in you.
A being profound, beyond thought and dream,
Yet they belittle, tear at your seam.
Do not let their voices shatter your core,
You are the ocean, not a wave on the shore.
Their eyes are veiled; they cannot perceive,
The depth of your spirit, the heights you achieve.
Your essence is boundless, your existence grand,
A force unbroken, a grain of stardust in hand.
Though others mock, their laughter unkind,
They cannot tarnish the gold in your mind.
For diamonds lie hidden beneath the dirt,
Their brilliance untarnished, immune to the hurt.
And so, your value, though unseen today,
Will rise like the sun, chasing shadows away.
Do not seek approval from those who are blind,
For greatness resides in a resolute mind.
Their words are but echoes, hollow and weak,
Your destiny waits for the bold to speak.

Stand tall in the storm, let the winds rage,
For every chapter turns another page.
The market may barter, they may weigh and trade,
But your worth is a light that will never fade.
Remember, the stars do not plead to shine,
They gleam in the darkness, forever divine.
So too, shall you, a beacon of grace,
Transcend the confines of time and space.
Let their doubts fuel the fire you hold,
Forge from their ashes a story bold.
For you are not a coin to be spent in haste,
But a melody eternal, with no time to waste.
Though the world may mock, and their eyes deceive,
You are more than their judgments conceive.
A soul infinite, with a purpose untold,
A being of wisdom, courageous and bold.
So rise from the market, shake off the dust,
Let the winds of change lift you with trust.
For you are priceless, a gem unrefined,
A force of nature, unconquered by time.

48. The Seven Tools of Destruction

The seven tools of destruction align,
Their edges sharp, their motives malign.
With whispers of ruin, they circle near,
To fracture your soul, to stoke your fear.
But hold firm, my friend, let courage prevail,
For faith, though small, can tip the scale.
A grain of sand in the tempest's tide,
Can anchor a heart, keep hope alive.
First comes the blade of doubt, so keen,
It cuts through dreams, unseen, obscene.
Yet doubt's sharp edge meets truth's bright shield,
And wavers before a mind that won't yield.
Second, the hammer of despair will fall,
To shatter your spirit, to break your call.
But despair cannot break what refuses to bow,
For faith rebuilds what despair disavows.
Third is the fire of rage untamed,
A scorching force, wild and unnamed.
Yet water flows steady, calm, and free,
Quelling the flames with humility.
Fourth is the net of greed, so vast,
Entangling those who cling to the past.

But contentment's blade cuts through the snare,

Leaving you light, with burdens rare.

Fifth comes the shadow of envy's might,

A blinding fog that dims the light.

Yet gratitude's glow can pierce the haze,

And set the envious heart ablaze.

Sixth is the wind of lies that howl,

A storm of deceit, relentless and foul.

But truth, though quiet, endures the gale,

Its whisper steadfast, its power prevails.

Seventh, the chains of fear constrict,

A weight too heavy, a force to inflict.

But courage blooms where fear takes root,

Breaking the chains with a resolute pursuit.

Together they conspire, these seven tools,

To bend your will, to make you their fool.

But as long as faith holds in your hand,

Even a grain can make you stand.

Faith is the fortress that cannot fall,

A shield against destruction's call.

It whispers, "Endure, for you are more,

Than the tools of ruin or their fateful roar."

Though the world may batter, bruise, and tear,

You are the craftsman, your soul to repair.

For destruction's tools are nothing but dust,

Before the resolve of a heart that trusts.

So stand your ground, let faith expand,

As vast as the ocean, as firm as the land.

The tools may strike, but they'll find no gain,

Against the power of your enduring grain.
The seven tools may try to shatter,
But faith will rise, for nothing else matters.
A grain of sand, a seed of belief,
Will grow into strength and grant you relief.
For you are the storm that cannot break,
The light that burns for its own sake.
Hold fast, my friend, through trials and strife,
For faith, though small, breathes infinite life.

49. The God of Your Destiny

Be with the crowd, yet apart in your soul,
A spark that defies, a fire untold.
Blend, if you must, in the sea of the known,
But let your light be uniquely your own.
Tread not the paths where others convene,
Where the footprints of many have already been.
The trodden road is a prison of thought,
But freedom is found where the world is not.
Forge your own trail through the wilderness wide,
Let courage and vision be your guide.
The world may mock, may brand you a fool,
But you write the script; you define the rule.
For greatness comes to those who dare,
To walk unknown roads without despair.
You are the sculptor, the canvas, the clay,
The god of your destiny, paving the way.
If they call you mad, let them scream,
For madness births the most daring dream.
The crowd may laugh, but laughter fades,
While your name will echo in the paths you've made.
Do not seek to mingle, to blur in the mass,
Be the gleaming shard in a sea of glass.
Patterns are comfort, repetition their creed,
But a mistake that stands out is what the world needs.

Be the note that breaks the melody's flow,
The river that bends where none dare to go.
For even a flaw in its boldest stride,
Can reshape the world and turn the tide.
Lead if you can, with a vision so clear,
Or follow with strength, but never with fear.
Let the crowd chase shadows, tethered to norms,
While you chase storms, redefining their forms.
You owe the world nothing; your purpose is yours,
Not bound by their rules, their fences, or doors.
Your worth is not measured by their acclaim,
But by the fire that burns in your name.
So rise, oh seeker, and claim your domain,
Break from the shackles, the bonds, and the chain.
Be not a replica, dull and confined,
But a masterpiece, bold and unrefined.
Be the thunder in a sky too quiet,
The rebel flame in a world of riot.
For life is not meant to fade or conform,
But to erupt in brilliance, a storm to transform.
The crowd will march to the drummer's beat,
But you are the symphony, fierce and complete.
They may never understand the paths you choose,
But in forging your own, there is nothing to lose.
So stand tall, my friend, and fear no scorn,
For legends are born where courage is sworn.
And when the crowd fades, as crowds always do,
Your path will remain, eternal and true.

Be not a follower, nor a sheep in the herd,
But the voice of the wild, the untamed word.
Be the question that challenges, the answer obscure,
A beacon of chaos, wild and pure.
For in the end, what matters is this:
Did you live in fear, or chase your bliss?
You are the god of your destiny's art,
So craft it with passion, and lead with your heart.

50. The Silent Healer

She hurt me so deeply, yet I did not bleed,
A wound unseen, but raw in its need.
My heart lay shattered, torn and bare,
Yet my lungs still drew the bitter air.
I cried with my eyes, a flood of despair,
But my lips stayed sealed, my voice nowhere.
I had lost so much, an empty core,
Yet still, I stood, ready to lose some more.
Life became a cruel, unyielding game,
Each day a trial, each breath the same.
The weight of sorrow, a relentless tide,
Threatened to pull me far from the light inside.
Then came a moment, a flicker, a spark,
A wagging tail cutting through the dark.
My dog appeared with a look so true,
Eyes asking, "What has happened to you?"
He pressed his nose to my trembling hand,
As if to say, "I understand."
No words were spoken, no speeches made,
Yet in his gaze, a hope conveyed.
"Is it worth your life for the one who fled,
Who left you cold, as good as dead?
Or will you rise for the many who stay,
Who long for you to greet each day?"

His question echoed, simple, profound,
Breaking the silence with no sound.
For in his wag, his gaze, his care,
I saw a love that was always there.
The world had seemed empty, cruel, and vast,
But his presence reminded me of joys past.
Of mornings bright, of laughter's refrain,
Of healing hearts and mending pain.
Life is more than the ones who depart,
It's the moments and beings who touch your heart.
A million souls may wait and yearn,
For your light to shine, for your fire to burn.
Pain may linger, its lessons unkind,
But love like his is easy to find.
In wagging tails, in loyal eyes,
In the simple truth that never lies.
So I rose that day, though battered and torn,
A phoenix emerging, reborn.
The pain still whispered, but it couldn't stay,
For love had led me a brighter way.
Not all who leave are meant to remain,
And not all loss should define your pain.
For life offers gifts in many a form,
A wagging tail, a heart so warm.
To those who hurt and those who heal,
To fleeting wounds and bonds that feel—
I found my strength, my purpose to live,
Through the silent love a dog could give.

So let the past be a bridge you cross,
Not an anchor that holds you to loss.
For every soul that walks away,
There are countless others who beg you to stay.
Rise for them, for yourself, for the light,
For the dawn that follows each longest night.
And when the world seems cruel and grim,
Look to the love that overflows its brim.
It may come wagging, it may come small,
But its power is boundless, it heals us all.
So breathe again, let the pain subside,
For love like that will always abide.

51. The Boundless Horizon

How to explore the horizon, when you cannot move?
How to chase the stars, when you've no room to prove?
The world stretches wide, an ocean of dreams,
But you are confined, it would seem.
How to move on when your feet are tied?
When your heart is bound, and your soul has died?
The chains are tight, the path unclear,
Yet still, the journey calls, loud and near.
How to breathe when submerged in the deep?
When silence reigns, and shadows creep?
The weight of the water, the pressure so cold,
Yet within you, a fire still unfolds.
Life places obstacles, a never-ending stream,
Mountains to climb, and rivers to dream.
Each step a struggle, each breath a fight,
But what if these struggles hold the light?
For obstacles are not walls, but doors yet unseen,
Hidden opportunities, quiet and keen.
When life feels heavy, when hope seems thin,
Look within, for the strength to begin.
You may be tied to a chair, unable to move,
But still, you can choose the path to improve.
In the stillness, find wisdom so vast,
The present moment holds the future's cast.

Your feet may be shackled, your spirit held tight,
But your mind can soar, like a bird in flight.
Every limitation is an invitation,
To break free, to find new foundation.
Under water, where breath is scarce,
Dive deeper, let the currents be your prayer.
The pressure may crush, the weight may drag,
But beneath the surface, there's no need to lag.
For in that stillness, the lesson is clear,
You are not bound by what you fear.
The horizon is not just what you see,
But what lies within, where you are free.
So how do you move when you're anchored in place?
You shift your perspective, slow down the race.
In stillness, find a rhythm unknown,
A pulse of life in a world overblown.
How do you explore when you cannot roam?
You turn inward, and make your mind a home.
The world may be vast, but your soul knows the way,
The horizon is not far, it's with you each day.
The obstacles you face are steps on a path,
A journey to wisdom, to conquer the wrath.
The water you breathe, the chair you endure,
They are the tools that will make you more sure.
In every challenge, there's a chance to grow,
To turn the storm's winds into a gentle flow.
For obstacles are not the end of the line,
But the beginning of something divine.

So when life binds you, don't shrink in despair,
Find the opportunities hidden with care.
For even in darkness, there's a spark to ignite,
A chance to rise, a chance to take flight.
How to explore the horizon, when you cannot move?
By understanding the power within you to improve.
How to move on, when you're tied to a chair?
By knowing that freedom is found everywhere.
How to breathe, when the waters are deep?
By trusting that life's lessons are yours to keep.
Turn the obstacles into stepping stones high,
And you'll find the horizon within your sky.

52. Beyond the Senses

How does color matter when I am blind?
When the world is dark, and sight is confined?
The hues of the rainbow, the shades of the sky,
All lost to the eyes, but not to the mind.
For within, there's a vision no eyes can see,
A world of thoughts, vast and free.
Though light may fade and darkness remain,
The soul still finds its path through the pain.
How does music matter when I am deaf?
When silence wraps around me, tight as a breath?
The melody lost, the rhythm away,
The notes unheard, yet still they stay.
For the heart has its own tune to play,
A song of love, of life, of yesterday.
The beats may fade, but the pulse remains,
A silent dance that breaks all chains.
How does life matter when I am dead?
When breath is still and the heart has fled?
The body rests, the soul is gone,
But does the story end with dawn?
For death is not the end of the tale,
It is but a whisper, a fleeting sail.
Life's true meaning is not in the span,
But in how we live, and the hearts we can.

It's in the love we give, the kindness we share,
The moments we live with thought and care.
It's in the silence and the song we create,
The peace we bring, the hands we take.
What is the worth of sight when it fades,
Or sound when it's lost in life's shades?
It's the unseen beauty, the unheard sound,
The love in the silence that still surrounds.
Colour may be gone, but not the grace,
For the world is bright in its own place.
Music may be silent, but the soul can sing,
A harmony that makes the heart take wing.
And when life feels empty, or death seems near,
Know that your spirit has nothing to fear.
For life is in how you've lived, not how long,
In the love you've given, in the heart's song.
So colour, music, life—each has its part,
But true beauty lives in the soul, the heart.
In moments, in actions, in dreams that flow,
In knowing the light that within you grows.
Live beyond the senses, beyond the pain,
For the essence of life is not in the gain.
It's in how you touch, how you love, how you stand,
In the ways you heal with your own hand.
Colour matters not to the blind who feel,
Music matters not to those who heal.
Life matters not to the one who's gone,
But the legacy remains, a lasting song.

So whether you see, or hear, or know,
The light of your spirit will always glow.
It's not in what's lost, but in what you give,
That makes life matter—how you choose to live.

53. Relentless Forward

As I walked along the beach, so vast and wide,
I watched the crabs, with scarlet shells, beside,
They scuttled toward the sea, with silent grace,
While egrets feasted, swift in their chase.
Yet the crabs, undaunted, pressed on through the fray,
Not swayed by the birds, nor the trials of the day.
For the sea, their home, was where they must be,
And so they moved forward, relentless and free.
Through the forest, where shadows whispered in light,
Bees hummed, with wings, in the quiet of night.
Around wild flowers, they buzzed with care,
Though their honeycomb broken, in the open air.
No sorrow could halt their tireless flight,
They gathered the nectar, in the glow of twilight.
For the sweetness of life, they sought and found,
In every flower, in every sound.
By the river, with waters flowing so deep,
Beavers worked hard, where shadows creep.
They built their dams, sturdy and strong,
Though humans destroyed them, time and again, wrong.
Yet they did not falter, nor shy away,
They built once more, at the break of day.
For the river was home, and the work was pure,
And nothing could stop them from enduring the lure.

In the fields, where the grains grow tall,
Rats scurried in silence, answering the call.
They gathered what they could, for the winter ahead,
Though their homes were destroyed, their futures misled.
They pressed on, undeterred by the loss,
Through fields and storms, they bore their cross.
For they knew the secret of life's sacred thread,
To keep moving forward, no matter the dread.
So let the winds howl, and the storms may rage,
Let the world turn, and time, like a cage,
Let others try to break you down,
Keep moving forward, with heart, not a frown.
For in the face of struggle, the strong will rise,
Like the crab to the sea, beneath open skies.
The bees, the beavers, the rats of the earth,
Show us the strength to find our worth.
For life's not a journey of ease and peace,
But a constant struggle that will never cease.
But in the face of hardship, let your spirit soar,
And like the creatures, rise, and rise once more.
For in each setback, there's a lesson to learn,
In each challenge, there's something to discern.
So walk the path with courage and might,
And keep moving forward, into the light.
Let your heart be strong, and your will unshaken,
No matter how many times you're taken.
For like the crabs, the bees, and the rats,
Resilience lies in overcoming all that's flat.
The world may break you, time and again,

But in your soul, there's strength to sustain.
So keep walking forward, through storm and flame,
For each step is progress, and none is in vain.

54. The Journey of a Raindrop

When raindrops fall from the boundless sky,
They know not where they'll fall, nor why.
Some land on dry sand, parched and bare,
Others on rocks, with no one to care.
Some quench the thirst of birds in flight,
While others kiss the plants with pure delight.
And some, perhaps, fall on a seashell's curve,
Turning into pearls with grace and nerve.
The possibilities stretch far and wide,
An endless path where fate may guide.
For each drop's journey, though unknown,
Teaches us lessons we can call our own.
Good or bad, the drop must fall,
It doesn't hesitate, doesn't stall.
Some may rise, some may sink in despair,
But none of them ever falter, nor dare
To question why they came or where they go,
They just move forward, letting the world flow.
The drops may fall in a stormy fight,
Or gently descend in the calm of the night.
But whether they crash or softly glide,
They all carry the same truth inside:
To live is to move, to grow, to strive,
To face the unknown, and continue to thrive.

So what if the path is dark and steep?
So what if promises are broken, and dreams we keep
Seem far out of reach, or lost in the air,
The raindrop moves, without a care.
It doesn't choose its place or time,
It only falls, its journey sublime.
So, too, must we in life's own storm,
Keep moving forward, no matter the form.
Whether we rise or whether we fall,
We must continue, through it all.
For the raindrop teaches a truth so clear,
To move ahead, without fear.
Like the raindrop, life's paths are unknown,
With twists and turns, yet we are never alone.
Sometimes, we falter, sometimes we soar,
But the key is simple, nothing more—
Keep moving on, with faith and grace,
For time will heal, and we'll find our place.
When the raindrops fall, so should we,
Embrace the unknown, and let it be.
Whether good or bad, rise or fall,
We move, we learn, we stand tall.
The journey's uncertain, but that's the way,
For we are the raindrops, here to stay.

55. The Shirt of Happiness

The king of the land, with wealth untold,
A kingdom of riches, and children bold,
A loving queen, and subjects dear,
Yet his heart was heavy, consumed by fear.
He had all the treasures one could see,
But happiness, to him, did not agree.
With gold and jewels, his halls adorned,
But in his soul, he was forlorn.
He longed for peace, for joy to come,
To fill the void, to quiet the drum
Of doubt and sorrow, always near,
Though everything else seemed crystal clear.
One day, a hermit, wise and old,
Came to the kingdom, stories untold.
He looked upon the king's deep pain,
And offered a solution, free from disdain.
"Seek the shirt of the happiest man,
And wear it, king, as your plan."
The king, intrigued, commanded his men,
To search the land, from then to then.
East and west, they went with haste,
To find the happiest man, in the human race.
They met with people, poor and weak,
Many had sorrow, and joy they did not seek.

Some had no children, some had no gold,
Some worked too hard, their lives uncontrolled.
Some were ill, some full of grief,
Yet none were happy, none found relief.
And then, in the distance, a song could be heard,
A melody sweet, a cheerful word.
A beggar sat, under the sky so blue,
Singing a tune, with a heart so true.
His clothes were ragged, his feet were bare,
But in his eyes, there was no despair.
The soldiers approached, with joy and surprise,
To see the beggar, with no sorrow in his eyes.
The king asked, "Are you the happiest of all?"
The beggar smiled, standing tall.
"Yes, I am happy," he said with glee,
"For there's no reason to be sad, you see."
The king, amazed, asked with grace,
"Then give me your shirt, to take its place."
The beggar laughed, a hearty sound,
"No shirt to give, none to be found!
For I wear no shirt, just my skin so free,
And in this freedom, I find my glee."
The king stood still, confused by the way,
The beggar lived with no dismay.
The joy was not in clothes or gold,
It came from within, and made him bold.
The king's heart stirred, as he came to know,
That happiness was not a thing to show.

It was not in riches, nor power's reign,
Not in possessions, nor in pain.
Happiness is found in a heart so light,
In accepting the moment, in living right.
The beggar's song, the king's new truth,
Taught him that joy is found in youth.
Not in the years, nor in the land,
But in the heart, where joy will stand.
The king returned to his palace grand,
With peace in his soul, and joy at hand.
For the shirt of happiness is not to find,
But in the freedom of a peaceful mind.
So when you search for joy, don't look afar,
It's found within, like a guiding star.
Like the beggar, who wore no shirt,
It's in letting go, and not in the hurt.
For happiness comes in simple ways,
In laughter, in song, in brighter days.

56. The Diya of Compassion

On the edge of a forest, beneath the skies so wide,
Bhola the woodcutter and Mira, his bride,
Lived humbly and kindly, with hearts pure and true,
In a hut made of dreams, where sunlight once flew.
It was Diwali night, the festival of light,
When joy filled the air and the world shone bright.
But in Bhola's small home, no riches were found,
Only a handful of rice on a table unbound.
Bhola returned, weary, no wood had he sold,
No coins in his pocket, no silver, no gold.
Mira, with love, had cooked what she could,
And they sat down together, their spirits withstood.
As dusk kissed the earth, the village came alive,
Houses adorned with lamps in a festive drive.
Bhola and Mira lit their lone diya with care,
Its flicker a whisper of hope in despair.
Then came a commotion, voices raised in the air,
A shadow approaching, a figure laid bare.
A girl in a shawl, so tattered and worn,
Her eyes held a sorrow too heavy, forlorn.
She stretched out her hand, her voice barely heard,
"Please, a morsel of food," she spoke the soft word.
Bhola and Mira looked, their hearts gripped with dread,
For her fingers were marred, her hands leprous and red.

Yet Mira, unshaken, with a heart warm and wide,
Took the girl's hand and gently drew her inside.
She washed her wounds with the care of a mother,
And fed her with love like none other.
"Stay for the night," Mira earnestly said,
But the girl shook her head, her path lay ahead.
"I have homes to visit, my journey goes on,"
And into the night, like a whisper, she was gone.
As Bhola and Mira turned back to their place,
A wonder awaited, a blessing, a grace.
For their hut had vanished, no longer it stood,
In its place was a mansion of stone and wood.
Rich garments adorned them, jewels bright and rare,
Their humble old clothes dissolved into air.
In awe, they knelt, tears streaming with light,
For they knew they were blessed on this sacred night.
Goddess Lakshmi had come in disguise so divine,
Testing their hearts with her silent sign.
Their kindness had shone like the brightest flame,
And blessings unbound to their doorstep came.
O traveller of life, take heed of this tale,
Kindness is a lantern that shall never pale.
For wealth is not gold, nor jewels, nor land,
But the warmth of a heart, the touch of a hand.
In the darkest of times, when shadows surround,
Let your diya of love in the world be found.
For the divine walks amongst us, silent and shy,
In the form of the weary, the poor passing by.

So light up your hearts as you light up the night,
With compassion and love, your truest delight.
And know that the universe watches your way,
Blessings will come, like the dawn to the day.

57. The Path We Share

What are you seeking, my friend, in the endless skies?
When all that you need lies before your eyes.
Pause for a moment, hear your heart's quiet call,
For the journey alone brings no joy at all.
The road stretches onward, a solitary track,
But what is the joy if no one has your back?
Let us walk together, hand in hand,
For life's greatest treasures aren't castles or land.
Think of the days when our laughter rang free,
Like ripples of sunlight that dance on the sea.
The wheels of our bicycles on deserted lanes,
The freedom of youth, no worries, no chains.
Remember the mangoes we plucked from the trees,
The thrill of the chase, the rustling breeze.
The splash of the river, cool waters so deep,
Where secrets were whispered and memories keep.
Oh, the joy of togetherness, simple and pure,
A bond forged in childhood, steadfast and sure.
For no riches compare, no treasures suffice,
To the warmth of a friendship that asks no price.
Yet here you are, seeking treasures unknown,
In distant lands, you wander alone.
But tell me, my friend, does the silence console?
Does the weight of the world not burden your soul?

The path may be long, the horizon unclear,
But together we walk, dispelling all fear.
For life is a journey, a song yet unsung,
Best shared with a friend when the heart is young.
One day the road may diverge, as it often does,
And we'll part with a smile, with love and trust.
But until that day, let's treasure the now,
And honor the past with a silent vow.
For the moments we shared are the treasures we keep,
The laughter, the tears, the dreams that we reap.
So what are you searching for, my dear friend?
The true wealth you seek lies where paths blend.
In the rustle of leaves, in the river's sweet song,
In the memories cherished, where we both belong.
The heart knows the truth, so stop and stay,
Let us walk together through life's fleeting day.
The stars will guide, the moonlight will show,
That the joy of companionship helps us to grow.
And when the journey ends, as all journeys do,
The path will remain, forever with you.
So take my hand, let's walk side by side,
Through life's open fields, let's share the ride.
For the world may change, but this truth is clear:
The heart finds its home when friendship is near.

58. Walk On, O Traveller

O traveller, don't halt, don't despair,
Though failure greets you with a daunting stare.
Each step you take, though steep or slow,
Is a path to the blooms where dreams will grow.
The road of life is not always kind,
Yet strength resides in your heart and mind.
Through thorny trails and shadows deep,
The treasures of triumph are yours to reap.
Opportunities rise like the morning sun,
A new chance begins when the old is done.
So walk on, stride bold, and face the strife,
For endless are the chances in the dance of life.
The path may wound, the stones may sting,
Yet onward lies where the flowers spring.
For no great feat was ever found,
Without first treading on rugged ground.
Someday the sun will bow to your will,
And the moon will glow as the night turns still.
The stars will weave a celestial song,
Celebrating the journey you traveled long.
When weariness weighs and tears might fall,
Pause for a moment, and recall it all.
The miles you've crossed, the mountains climbed,
The victories seized in moments unprimed.

Look not behind to mourn the loss,
But ahead to the bridge you're yet to cross.
For each failure, a lesson unfolds,
A gift of wisdom more precious than gold.
Embrace the night, for it whispers near,
That dawn is closer, there's nothing to fear.
Through every storm and every trial,
You build a strength that stays a while.
So walk on, O traveller, lift your chin,
For every ending hides a new begin.
Life is the path; you're its guiding flame,
Write your story with passion and name.
For only through thorns do roses bloom,
And only through dusk does the daylight loom.
Carry your dreams like a lantern bright,
To light the shadows and conquer the night.
And when you're tired, let the echo remind,
How far you've come with a fearless mind.
The road ahead is your grand design,
Walk on, O traveller—your stars will shine.

59. The Beauty of Simplicity

In a world where dreams chase skies of gold,
Lies a secret story, quietly told.
Of simple joys, so pure, so true,
Where life's small wonders paint the view.
A modest home, with walls of care,
Where love and laughter fill the air.
Three humble meals, a feast to savor,
Each bite a token of nature's favor.
The morning sun, a golden hue,
Whispers promises fresh and new.
A walk through fields where breezes play,
Greets the soul at the break of day.
But man, bewitched by glitter's gleam,
Forgets the charm of a simple dream.
He runs through mazes, built by pride,
Chasing shadows, far and wide.
He builds tall towers, he craves for fame,
Seeks to etch in time his fleeting name.
Power, success—a mirage they seem,
Fading fast like a fleeting dream.
The more he earns, the less he gains,
The price is paid in silent pains.
For what is wealth if peace departs,
And restlessness weighs heavy hearts?

In gardens small, where flowers bloom,
Lies freedom from the world's loud gloom.
Where chirping birds in chorus sing,
And happiness resides in everything.
The child who laughs with carefree joy,
The elder who rests without employ,
Teach us lessons we fail to see,
That less is more, and more is free.
Oh, seeker, pause your hurried stride,
Look around at life, let your heart decide.
Does gold outweigh the morning breeze?
Can power rival the swaying trees?
For every sunrise gently reminds,
The richest treasure is peace of mind.
No throne nor crown, no fame, no race,
Can match the warmth of love's embrace.
The secret lies in letting go,
Of endless wants and tales of woe.
Contentment blooms where greed retreats,
And joy walks lightly on humble feet.
So simplify, and shed the weight,
That binds your soul to a restless fate.
Find bliss in moments, quiet and still,
And learn the art of a life fulfilled.
For when the sun sets on life's shore,
We'll crave not riches, but moments more.
A simple house, a meal, a song,
Were all we needed all along.

60. A Journey With Yourself

When days grow quiet, and shadows fall,
When no one lingers, no one calls,
The world will hum its endless tune,
While you sit beneath the silvery moon.
Fear not the silence, nor the still,
For life unfolds its gentle will.
Companions fade, and time moves on,
Yet in your heart, you're never alone.
Speak to the birds, their songs so bright,
They'll serenade you in morning light.
Whisper to trees with arms outstretched,
Their wisdom deep, their roots far-fetched.
Let animals teach their simple ways,
In their presence, find gentle days.
The plants will bloom, their colours true,
They'll share their quiet joy with you.
Pick up a brush, let your heart create,
Paint your dreams, it's never too late.
Each stroke a story, each hue a voice,
In art, you'll find your inner choice.
Sing a song, let the echoes rise,
Lift your spirit to the open skies.
The melody will guide your feet,
As you wander where the earth and heavens meet.

Take long walks on the paths untamed,
Feel the wind, let it call your name.
Each step a rhythm, a steady beat,
Each mile a treasure, a world complete.
For now is the time, this moment, this place,
To honor yourself, to slow the race.
You are the sun, the stars, the sea,
A universe vast in simplicity.
Do not despair when you're on your own,
For solitude is a seed well-sown.
In quiet moments, the soul will bloom,
A garden of peace in life's grand room.
Seek not the crowd to fill the void,
Nor chase the fleeting, the world's decoyed.
The truest bond you'll ever find,
Is the love you share with your own mind.
When age arrives, and youth has fled,
When laughter echoes from years you've led,
You'll find a friend in the mirror's gaze,
A kindred spirit through all your days.
So cherish the now, the life within,
The journeys waiting to begin.
For when all else fades, you'll come to see,
You are your best company.

61. A Silent Elegy

Winters are no longer cold,
Their breath of frost no longer bold.
The snow that whispered tales of yore,
Has vanished now, forevermore.
Summers rage like an unchained flame,
The earth itself has lost its name.
The shade once offered by trees so grand,
Is now but dust, a barren land.
Spring, a ghost, a fleeting dream,
A figment born of memory's stream.
No blossoms bloom, no fragrance sways,
Just faded echoes of brighter days.
The banyan tree, my sacred retreat,
Where roots ran deep and life would meet,
Is gone, its shade no longer cast,
Its trunk a memory of the past.
Children no longer laugh and play,
Amidst its roots in the heat of day.
Hide and seek, their joyous cheer,
Replaced by silence, stark and clear.
The lanes once bustling, alive with sound,
Now wide, deserted, hollow ground.
For every soul is locked away,
With screens to guide their fleeting day.

Fingers dance on lifeless glass,
While life itself is left to pass.
Eyes transfixed by a flickering glow,
Ignoring the world we used to know.
The forests fall, their whispers die,
No rustling leaves, no canopy sky.
The axe has carved its cruel decree,
And silenced songs of the ancient tree.
The rivers shrink, their voices weak,
Their once-bold currents now barely speak.
The birds have flown, their nests unmade,
Their songs replaced by a digital parade.
Technology, with its siren's call,
Promised to lift us, yet made us fall.
It stitched the world with wires unseen,
Yet tore apart what might have been.
The banyan's loss, the forest's wane,
Mirror the soul's unspoken pain.
What price this progress, this endless speed,
If it feeds our wants but kills our need?
To touch, to feel, to breathe, to see,
To sit beneath a living tree.
To hear the laughter of a child,
To walk in forests deep and wild.
But now we sit in glowing rooms,
Each one a self-created tomb.
Connections lost, though wires abound,
A hollow silence, a deafening sound.

The earth, once vibrant, bold, and free,
Now bends beneath our tyranny.
The banyan's roots no longer sprawl,
And with it, life begins to fall.
Perhaps one day, when skies grow bare,
When nothing's left but poisoned air,
We'll long for winters crisp and cold,
And summers less a tale of old.
We'll mourn the banyan, the forest's heart,
The role we played in their depart.
And maybe then, through grief's embrace,
We'll strive to heal this wounded place.
But until then, the screen still hums,
A lullaby of what we've become.
And in its glow, we fail to see,
The cost of what is now debris.
The banyan waits in silent plea,
A symbol of what used to be.
Its shade a memory, its roots untold,
A tragedy born of progress bold.
The earth endures, though scarred and torn,
Its beauty faded, its spirit worn.
Yet hope remains in hearts that fight,
To reclaim the dark and restore the light.

62. When I Waited for You

I waited for you beneath the weary moon,
As stars whispered secrets to the silent dune.
Each breath I took was a prayer in disguise,
A longing etched deep in my tear-laden eyes.
The clock hands circled, mocking my despair,
Time unraveled dreams I thought we would share.
But you never came, though I hoped you might,
The weight of absence darkened my night.
I wove my love into letters so true,
Sealed with tears that only bled for you.
Each word a whisper, a fragment of me,
Cast adrift on a tempestuous sea.
Yet now, when my shadow has fled from the shore,
When the echoes of love knock no more,
You clutch the pillow, haunted by pain,
Reading my letters again and again.
You sit by the window, your gaze turned to dust,
Hoping for miracles, a love that must.
But not every belief blooms into light,
Some seeds of hope wither in the night.
For I have wandered through love's winding maze,
Through endless tunnels and blinding haze.
And there I learned, to my aching dismay,
That love is a folly that leads hearts astray.

Yet even in sorrow, a truth I have found,
That love must be nurtured on worthy ground.
Not scattered like leaves on the winds of chance,
Nor burned by the flames of a fleeting glance.
I care to love someone who truly sees,
Who walks through the storms and steadies my seas.
Who holds not my letters but holds my hand,
And builds with me dreams that together will stand.
So while you wait through endless nights,
Clutching the past in desperate fights,
Know that some roads do not return,
And some candles, once out, cease to burn.
Do not hold on to a fading star,
Seek the light where true hearts are.
For love is not in the ache of despair,
But in the warmth of someone who's there.
Still, I wish for you peace, a gentle release,
From the chains of longing, a chance to cease.
For though I am gone, my care still flows,
In the quiet of dreams, where memory glows.
So bid me farewell, let the letters lie,
Seek a new dawn beneath the vast sky.
For love's truest form is not in the wait,
But in the courage to rewrite fate.

63. The Silent Giver

Without my asking, You gave me so much,
Yet my lips held no prayer, no grateful touch.
What I sought, You withheld from my hand,
But every true need, You made sure to stand.
You never gave me a crutch to lean,
Instead, You stayed distant, unseen.
From afar, You watched me rise and fall,
Teaching me to walk, despite it all.
In shadows deep, You lit no flame,
Yet courage within, You helped me claim.
The meaning of Your ways, beyond my reach,
Yet every wound held a lesson to teach.
I thought I was abandoned, left to stray,
But You cleared my path in Your quiet way.
The pride I held, You softly broke,
In every loss, a blessing You spoke.
When I stumbled, You offered no hand,
But gave me the strength to firmly stand.
You hid the answers, cloaked in time,
Yet in every trial, I found the sublime.
I asked for joy; You sent me strife,
To teach me the value of a meaningful life.
I begged for ease; You sent me pain,
So I'd find growth in every strain.

Your silence spoke louder than words,
In the quiet, I heard the wisdom of birds.
You took what I clung to, held so dear,
And left me with peace, so bright and clear.
I thought I was broken, lost in despair,
Yet every wound healed, with Your care.
The solace I sought was not in Your hand,
But in the strength You helped me command.
Each unanswered plea was a hidden grace,
Each denied wish brought me to this place.
I craved Your shelter; You gave me rain,
To teach me endurance through every pain.
In every fall, I learned to rise,
With clearer vision through tear-filled eyes.
You taught me to walk, You taught me to stand,
Without ever taking me by the hand.
Now I see the gifts You bestow,
In every high, in every low.
For every dream that never came true,
A greater purpose was crafted by You.
I've learned to trust in what I cannot see,
For every closed door shaped the key.
Your ways are hidden, but Your love is vast,
A guiding light, in every shadow You cast.
In my silence, I now find prayer,
In my struggle, I feel You there.
No need for words, no need for plea,
Your wisdom unfolds, setting me free.

The pain, the loss, the unanswered call,
Were steps in the journey, meant for my all.
For without the storm, the sky won't clear,
Without the trials, strength won't appear.
Now I thank You, not for what I sought,
But for the wisdom every trial brought.
For the gift of walking my path alone,
Yet never truly being on my own.
You gave me more than I ever knew,
A life reshaped, my spirit anew.
And so I walk, with my head held high,
Grateful for You, unseen in the sky.

64. Hail, O King of Jarbi

Hail, O King of Jarbi, whose crown now rusts,
Why dost thou tremble, why forsake thy trust?
Come forth, thou spirit of dread encased,
For I am the shadow thou once embraced.
They have adorned me in garlands of fear,
Praised my darkness from toe to hair.
Their whispers rise like a ghostly choir,
Calling thee forth to the pyre of fire.
Smitten with wrath, thou hast wandered too far,
Beyond the reach of thy guiding star.
The night is heavy with silence so deep,
Even the gods above dare not weep.
The stars are stripped, their light grown dim,
The trees stand hollow, their shadows grim.
No heaven opens its gates tonight,
But Hades looms with consuming might.
Beware, O King, for the fates conspire,
To kindle the flames of thy heart's desire.
Dost thou seek power, dost thou seek fame?
Or dost thou come to relinquish thy name?
For the night speaks truths thou cannot deny,
Each whisper a shard that pierces the sky.
It beckons thee near, with promises sweet,
Yet hides an abyss beneath thy feet.

Do not mistake the silence for peace,
It masks a storm that shall never cease.
The winds shall howl, the earth shall quake,
As the curse of thy greed begins to wake.
The spirits stir in their shadowed lair,
To mock thy pride, to strip thee bare.
They clutch at the edges of thy fraying crown,
Eager to pull thee, trembling, down.
Come take the substance thy soul requires,
Step forth, O King, to the blazing pyres.
Let the dark consume thy mortal frame,
And echo thy name in endless shame.
The night is thick, a suffocating shroud,
And the moon, a ghost, hides behind a cloud.
The air is laced with a chilling dread,
As the ground turns soft with the weight of the dead.
Canst thou not hear their mournful cries,
Rising like smoke to the ashen skies?
Their sorrow clings to thy regal thread,
A tapestry woven with the blood of the dead.
Repent, O King, while thou hast the chance,
Or risk eternal in Hades' dance.
For once the clock strikes the final hour,
No prayers can shield thee from its power.
Thy throne is built on a fragile lie,
A kingdom doomed beneath its sky.
Thy scepter shakes, thy rule grows thin,
For the end begins where pride has been.

The winds grow colder, the forest moans,
The shadows creep through the broken stones.
And thou, O King, must choose thy path,
Face thy doom, or escape its wrath.
Hail, O King, the night draws near,
The stars lay bare, the trees threadbare.
No heavens open to thy command,
But Hades stands, close at hand.
If thou dost not repent, thy fate is set,
And thou shalt have no chance to regret.
Come forth, O King, and meet thy fear,
For thy end, O King, is now so near.

65. If I Were Something Else

What if I were something else, not bound by form,
An eagle soaring high above, defying every storm?
With wings that cut through clouds, so strong and free,
I'd watch the world below, its beauty calls to me.
I'd trace the rivers winding paths, their endless flow,
See mountains kissed by sunlight, capped with snow.
The skies would be my kingdom, vast and wide,
Each moment pure and fleeting, my heart's true guide.
Or what if I were a whale, the ocean's king,
With songs that echo deep, a soulful hymn I'd sing?
I'd breach the waves in triumph, a thunderous spray,
Then dive to secret depths, where shadows softly lay.
Through coral cities vibrant, where silence holds,
I'd roam where ancient mysteries quietly unfold.
Each ripple tells a story, each tide a gentle sigh,
A dance of timeless wonders, beneath the boundless sky.
Perhaps I'd be a stag, swift as the rushing stream,
Leaping through the forest, living nature's dream.
Each hoofstep on the earth, a rhythm pure and true,
The forest would be my temple, bathed in morning dew.
From glades to shaded groves, my spirit would roam,
Each path a journey new, each clearing a home.
No fear, no chains to bind, just freedom's song,
A life of endless wonder, where I truly belong.

Or could I be a bee, so small, yet so divine,
Drinking nectar sweet and golden, from the sunshine?
I'd hum a tune of spring, a melody of cheer,
Flitting from bloom to bloom, each moment crystal clear.
Each flower would be my world, a paradise small,
In every petal's curve, life's beauty stands tall.
The dance of wings in sunlight, a hymn of grace,
Life's joy in simplest moments, time cannot erase.
Yet what would it mean, to leave behind this shell,
To not know human burdens, nor stories to tell?
No weight of expectation, no tasks to ever bear,
Just the call of nature, and freedom everywhere.
But would I trade this form, with all its heavy load,
For paths where love and meaning are not sowed?
The eagle soars in silence, alone in endless skies,
The whale sings songs unanswered, as fleeting time flies.
The stag runs free in shadows, yet solitude it knows,
The bee works ceaselessly, as fleeting seasons go.
Each life is painted richly, yet lacks the human spark,
The light of shared existence, that shines against the dark.
For burdens carve our spirits, and trials make us strong,
In struggle lies the music, of life's most vibrant song.
To dream, to hope, to rise despite the fall,
These are gifts of being human, the greatest of all.
So while I dream of other forms, I still embrace,
The beauty of this journey, the trials we face.
For in each weight I carry, there's wisdom to be found,
A strength born of endurance, a joy that's unbound.

If I were something else, I'd marvel at the view,
But still, I'd long for humankind, and all that we pursue.
For though the road is heavy, and shadows sometimes stay,
The light within the human soul can never fade away.

66. The Story of Mary Hattfinger

In the quiet cold of a moonlit night,

Mary Hattfinger sits, beneath the pale starlight.

Her fingers dance on keys, a rhythmic refrain,

Each word a window to her joy and pain.

She writes a tale, her biography unfolds,

A life of heavy burdens, secrets untold.

Remorse shadows her, betrayal cuts deep,

Yet within her heart, her dreams still leap.

By day, a receptionist, she greets with a smile,

Tirelessly working, mile upon mile.

No complaints escape her lips, no sighs, no tears,

She faces the world, suppressing her fears.

By night, she sits with her frugal fare,

A meal so simple, but she doesn't despair.

Her typewriter waits, her solitary friend,

Its soft tick-ticking, a comfort to the end.

Each word she types is a step she takes,

Through memories tender, through heartbreaks.

Her life becomes pages, black ink on white,

A novel emerging from the depths of night.

The betrayal that stung, the trust that was lost,

The bridges she burned, and the painful cost.

Yet Mary won't falter, she won't let it win,
For in her typewriter's rhythm, she finds life begin.
She pens her remorse, each regret laid bare,
The shadows of choices she cannot repair.
But in those shadows, a spark does gleam,
A whisper of hope, a lingering dream.
The selfish world may turn away,
But Mary's resolve will never sway.
For she knows her voice, her truth, her song,
And in the clatter of keys, she belongs.
She writes of struggle, of battles she's faced,
Of moments in darkness, of dreams misplaced.
But woven between are threads of gold,
Her triumphs, her joys, her courage bold.
Each chapter she crafts is a testament,
To a life lived fully, to energy spent.
She builds her story, brick by brick,
Through the nights long hours, tick by tick.
For the world may be selfish, harsh, and unkind,
But within her soul, she's clarity defined.
The typewriter whispers, "Go on, be free,"
And Mary becomes who she's meant to be.
Her story is hers, it belongs to no one,
Each word a battle, each page a sun.
She'll finish her novel, her truth will outshine,
A masterpiece born of her will divine.
Mary Hattfinger, a name carved in fate,
Proof that it's never too early or late.
To rise from the ashes, to claim what is true,

To find the strength that's hidden in you.
So let the keys clatter, let the ink run dry,
Mary won't stop; she won't say goodbye.
Her story's her beacon, her words her fight,
She writes through the cold, through the still of night.
And when the last line is typed, she'll stand tall,
A testament to rising after the fall.
Her life, though burdened, a victory cries,
For in her own words, her spirit flies.

67. In a Room of Time

Confined within walls, twelve feet by twelve,
Where silence echoes, where shadows delve.
A small window offers but a fleeting view,
Yet within, a universe waits to break through.
No phone, no distractions, no calls to take,
Just the tick of time, as it gently breaks.
A bulb hangs low, casting its dim light,
And I stand alone in the quiet of night.
What shall I do, in this room so still?
How will I fill the hours, against my will?
I could draw on the walls, with chalk in hand,
A landscape of dreams, a faraway land.
Or perhaps I'll write, let my thoughts take flight,
Spilling on paper, from morning to night.
The rhythm of words, the dance of rhyme,
Transforming the silence, making it sublime.
I may doodle patterns, shapes in the air,
A map of my mind, drawn without care.
Each swirl a release, each line a sigh,
In this room, my imagination can fly.
The lizards, they scurry along the wall,
Their tiny feet making no sound at all.
I'll talk to them softly, tell them my thoughts,
In this solitude, even silence is sought.

The spiders creep slowly, their webs they weave,
I watch with wonder, as I quietly breathe.
The world may be small, but the lessons are grand,
Even in a room, I'll find a way to stand.
Perhaps I'll sing a song, a melody sweet,
Let the notes carry me to a distant street.
The sound fills the air, a sweet lullaby,
A reminder that joy is found in the sky.
I may mimic voices, create a new tone,
In this room, I'll never feel alone.
For my mind is a canvas, endless and wide,
A treasure of thoughts, I carry inside.
You may call me mad, but I've found my way,
In the simplest moments, I choose to stay.
For boredom is only a prison we build,
With walls of thought, where dreams are stilled.
But I have learned to be resourceful, to see,
That even in stillness, there's endless glee.
The hours may crawl, but I'll make them fly,
In the silence of time, I'll touch the sky.
A room, a bulb, a small window's light,
Can hold infinite worlds if I choose to ignite.
For freedom is not just in places we roam,
But in the thoughts we carry, wherever we're home.
So while I am confined, I am never truly bound,
For in my own mind, I am always unbound.
The world is vast, yet here I will stay,
And fill the moments with light every day.

In a room, a life can be lived so free,
In the heart of silence, there's so much to see.
It's not in the walls that I find my strife,
But in the way I choose to live my life.

68. The Battle Within

Through fire and ruin, through blood and sand,
A war is waged by heart and hand.
Not just on fields where cannons cry,
But in the soul where shadows lie.
A soldier stands at duty's gate,
Bound by honor, sealed by fate.
Yet in his eyes, the battles roar—
One for country, one for home once more.
The trenches weep in silent screams,
Ghosts of men lost in their dreams.
A mother prays, a child still waits,
A house stands still, though time negates.
Across the dunes where sun burns red,
Lie bones of warriors long since dead.
Once they charged with swords held high,
Now wind-blown dust is their reply.
The jungles hum with whispers low,
Tales of those who came and go.
The trees, once green, now charred remain,
Bearing scars of man's disdain.
Through no man's land of shattered ground,
Where craters deep in sorrow drown,
A single rose in ruins grew—
A tale of loss, a hope so true.

Cities crumble, towers fall,
History fades upon each wall.
Once they sang with voices bright,
Now silence reigns through endless night.
The mountain peaks, once gods did tread,
Now watch as men paint valleys red.
Snow untouched by hands of time,
Witnessing glories lost in crime.
But wars of flesh are not the test,
The greatest war lies in the chest.
The ego whispers, fear takes hold,
A man once bright now withered cold.
Many gods have walked as men,
Fought with steel, yet fought within.
Crowned as kings, but in the end,
They too would break, they too would bend.
To win the war, not blade but soul,
Must learn to break, yet still be whole.
Not all who conquer lands and seas,
Have conquered self—such victories deceive.
A sword may pierce, a bomb may fall,
Yet man is prisoner to his call.
To fight for peace, to fight for pride,
Yet longing still, with hearts denied.
The battle rages, hour by hour,
Between the throne and fleeting power.
Between the beast and man confined,
Between the soul and troubled mind.

And so the war will never cease,
Though war itself may call for peace.
For while men breathe and hearts still burn,
The battle within must still be won.

69. The Colours Beyond Sight

If I were blind, how would I see
The colours of the world, so wild and free?
How would I know the red of a rose,
Or the green of the leaves as the soft wind blows?
Would I feel the warmth of the sun on my face,
But never know its golden embrace?
How would I tell the difference between night and day,
When darkness and light blend in endless gray?
I can smell the earth, the sweet perfume,
I can hear the song of a bird in bloom.
I can touch the soft petals, the rough bark of trees,
But how will I know what each color truly means?
For me, the world is a canvas unseen,
A landscape that's formless, forever serene.
No vibrant hues, no sparkling skies,
Only the whispers of the world, with closed eyes.
What would it be like to live without sight,
When colours are shadows in the heart's quiet night?
Would I yearn for a glimpse, a single view,
To see the blue sky, the ocean's true hue?
But perhaps there's a lesson, a truth to be found,
In a world where sight is not all around.

For colours are not just seen with the eyes,
They live in the heart, they breathe in the skies.
I may not see the rainbow's arc,
But I can feel its presence in the dark.
Each color has a rhythm, a pulse, a song,
And I'll learn to hear where they belong.
The red of passion, the green of life,
Are not just seen—they're felt in strife.
The blue of calm, the yellow of cheer,
Are woven in the air, they're always near.
I can't paint a picture with brush or hue,
But I can paint a life, with feelings true.
Each moment is a canvas, each breath a stroke,
And in the silence, there's meaning we provoke.
Dreams may not be colored, but they still shine bright,
For in my heart, I see their light.
And in my soul, the world is clear,
Not in color, but in the love I hold near.
Though the world is dark, I'm not without sight,
For my world is filled with a different light.
It's in the sounds, the scents, the touch,
It's in the depth of life, the beauty we clutch.
And perhaps, in this life without visual grace,
I find colours in every touch, every place.
For sight is but one way to see the world,
And in my blindness, life is unfurled.
So I may never know the blue of the sea,
But I will know the warmth it brings to me.
I'll feel the sun on my skin, so bright,

And know its color without seeing its light.
I may not see the world in shades so grand,
But I'll know its beauty by what I can stand.
And though I walk through the world in dark,
I'll leave behind a luminous spark.
For colours are not just what the eye perceives,
They live in the heart, in the world that believes.
In silence, in touch, in dreams we hold dear,
In the world of the blind, the colours are clear.

70. A Journey Unfathomed

How long I've traveled, I do not know,
Nor the reason why my steps must go.
No fatigue clings to this wandering soul,
No hunger or thirst to take its toll.
The path ahead, a wondrous view,
Each step a chapter, fresh and new.
No burdens weigh upon my stride,
No worldly ties to pull or bind.
Through forests dense with whispered trees,
Where leaves sway gently in the breeze,
Through mountains proud, their heads held high,
Piercing the clouds, embracing the sky.
Across the desert, vast and bare,
Under the sun's relentless glare,
Through meadows lush with blossoms bright,
Drenched in the glow of morning light.
Fields and farms where workers toil,
Breaking sweat on fertile soil,
Their hands at labor, their hearts in song,
A rhythm of life that moves along.
I pass them by, a silent guest,
Observing life at its vibrant best.
They bear their loads, they tend their flames,
Engraving purpose in life's great frame.

But I, a wanderer, free as air,
Have no chains of duty to ensnare.
No responsibilities weigh me down,
No cries of duty, no royal crown.
And yet, in my heart, a question stirs,
A yearning deep, though undefined, it purrs.
Why do I walk? What calls my name?
Is it the journey or some destined flame?
Perhaps it's the stars that light my path,
Whispering secrets of aftermath,
Or the winds that murmur soft and low,
Urging my restless feet to go.
The world is vast, its wonders many,
Each moment rich, its treasures plenty.
To walk is to breathe, to live, to see,
To embrace life's boundless mystery.
No maps to guide, no plans to make,
No fears to mend, no hearts to break.
Each step I take is mine alone,
Each moment fleeting, yet fully known.
So, onward I march through the unknown,
Through lands untouched, through seeds unsown.
In the simplicity of this endless quest,
I find my peace, my place of rest.
For life itself is the grandest tale,
A ship unmoored that sets its sail.
To wander is not to be lost, I see,
But to dance with the winds and eternity.

Let others labor, build, and strive,
Their efforts noble, their dreams alive.
But as for me, I'll simply roam,
For every step, I am already home.

71. The Song of the Complainer

To those who complain, with ceaseless cries,
Who see only clouds in the bluest skies,
Who find in sunshine an aching glare,
And in sweet rain, a burden to bear.
They lament their fate, they wail their plight,
Though their tables are full and their halls alight.
Rich to the bone, with treasures untold,
Yet stingy of heart, their kindness cold.
Their wealth, a fortress, built so high,
But no joy gleams in their guarded eye.
For gold may glimmer, and jewels may shine,
Yet they hoard their riches like a sacred shrine.
"Oh, woe is me!" they endlessly sigh,
As the seasons change and the years roll by.
Their coffers overflow, their vaults abound,
Yet they claim they're losing on every ground.
No gift they give, no smile they share,
No thought for others, no act of care.
Their hearts grow heavy, their spirits wane,
For wealth alone cannot ease the pain.
They grumble in summer, they grieve in spring,
They scoff at the joy each season brings.

When autumn's gold cloaks the weary earth,
They see decay, not nature's rebirth.
In winter's hush, when the world is still,
They shiver and moan against the chill.
Blind to beauty, deaf to song,
Their days of complaining stretch so long.
But one day, perhaps, they'll pause and see,
The futility of their misery.
For life's grand truth, both simple and wise,
Eludes the grasp of their selfish cries.
They'll learn that gold, though it gleams so bright,
Cannot buy peace, nor love, nor light.
That wealth is fleeting, a paper throne,
A fragile empire that stands alone.
The joy they seek, the solace they crave,
Is not in what they hoard or save.
But in the hearts they touch, the love they spread,
The hands they help, the mouths they've fed.
For life is brief, a flickering flame,
Not meant for grumbling, nor chasing fame.
Its treasures lie in the deeds we sow,
In the light we share, the kindness we show.
So to the complainers, a truth profound:
Stop chasing shadows, look around.
The world is vast, with wonders divine,
Far richer than coins or glittering shine.
Let go of grief, let go of disdain,
Embrace the sunshine, dance in the rain.
For every moment, however small,

Is a gift of life, the greatest of all.
And when they realize, as all must do,
That wealth fades away, but love is true,
They'll see that their complaints were vain,
And find in their hearts a sweeter refrain.
The song of life, so pure, so clear,
Will silence the grumbles they held dear.
And they'll know at last, beyond all measure,
The real wealth lies in life's simple treasure.

72. The Companions of Ink and Page

Oh, pen and paper, my truest friends,
On you my journey of thought depends.
You give me wings, a boundless flight,
To soar through realms of day and night.
When solitude wraps its quiet shroud,
You speak for me amidst the crowd.
Your silent whispers, your gentle grace,
Turn empty spaces to a sacred place.
Each stroke of ink, each line I write,
Reveals my soul in black and white.
Through your embrace, my heart is shown,
In words that feel like seeds I've sown.
How many times have I sought your aid,
When life's great trials left me dismayed?
Countless moments, I've poured my soul,
And found in writing, a way to be whole.
Through paper white, my thoughts cascade,
Flowing from heart where dreams are made.
Through veins unseen, through silent streams,
You help me decipher my deepest dreams.
In your presence, I find my voice,
A melody shaped by my heart's choice.

Each letter crafted, a bridge of grace,
To thoughts unknown, to a hidden space.
No burden too heavy, no tale too steep,
You hold my secrets, my joys, my grief.
You listen softly, without demand,
Your canvas open, your touch so grand.
Through you, I've wandered lands untold,
Built castles of words, and mines of gold.
You've captured stars, and morning dew,
And painted sunsets in every hue.
Amidst the noise of bustling days,
You guide me through life's tangled maze.
You echo back what I can't explain,
Turning my chaos into refrain.
A million lines, a thousand nights,
A journey woven through black ink's flight.
Each word a mirror, each phrase a spark,
Illuminating the shadows dark.
To hold a pen is to hold a key,
To the vault of thought, to eternity.
With every scribble, I learn anew,
What it means to feel, to dream, to do.
You've taught me the art of letting go,
To spill the burdens I may not show.
In your embrace, I find my peace,
A moment where all struggles cease.
And when the world seems vast and lone,
I find in you a kindred tone.
For in your silence, I hear a song,

A timeless anthem, steady and strong.
So here's to you, my steadfast pair,
To the pen and paper, always there.
You are my anchor, my guiding flame,
My truest allies, in life's great game.
Through you, I've learned what it means to feel,
To shape the void, to dream and heal.
Forever I'll cherish your gentle might,
My constant companions, by day and night.

73. From Concrete Jungles to Verdant Bliss

I stayed too long where the buildings grew,

A concrete jungle, a prison's hue.

The city roared with ceaseless strife,

A grind that drained the soul of life.

Noise filled the air, no birds in flight,

No stars adorned the velvet night.

Honking cars, a crowd's parade,

A life of haste, where dreams decayed.

The streets were rivers, choked with sound,

Where restless feet would pound and pound.

Eyes fixed on screens, no glance to spare,

For human warmth was seldom there.

No trees to shade, no flowers to bloom,

The air grew thick with urban gloom.

No squirrels played, no cows in sight,

Just stray dogs barking through the night.

I wore myself to the bone each day,

Chasing dreams that slipped away.

And in that rush, my heart grew cold,

Yearning for peace, for tales untold.

So, I resolved to leave behind,

The city's chains that bound my mind.

To seek a land where time stood still,
Where life aligned with nature's will.
I traveled far to the countryside,
Where mountains kissed the heavens wide.
The air was pure, the skies were blue,
And every breeze felt fresh and new.
The village lay in a tranquil vale,
With meadows lush and winding trails.
Fields of gold and rivers clear,
Where life was simple, kind, sincere.
The villagers, with hearts so kind,
Shared their stories, peace of mind.
They knew no rush, no frantic race,
Their smiles adorned this sacred place.
I built my home from timber strong,
Where birds would greet me with their song.
Each dawn was painted in hues of gold,
A masterpiece for the soul to hold.
The goats would graze, the cattle roam,
And every creature found a home.
The chickens clucked, the sparrows flew,
The stars returned, the night renewed.
I tilled the earth with my bare hands,
Felt the embrace of fertile lands.
The soil was rich, the harvest sweet,
A symphony of life complete.
No screens, no calls, no endless grind,
But books and thoughts to soothe the mind.
The mountains stood like ancient seers,

Their wisdom erasing all my fears.
The streams would laugh, the trees would dance,
Each moment offered a second chance.
The forest whispered secrets old,
Of love and joy and courage bold.
I watched the sunset paint the skies,
A fleeting gift before my eyes.
The stars would gather, soft and bright,
Their glow a balm to heal the night.
No longer bound by urban chains,
I found a life where beauty reigns.
No honking horns, no crowded street,
Just tranquil songs and hearts that beat.
The village taught me truths profound,
That happiness is simply found.
Not in the chase, nor wealth's parade,
But in the quiet, where dreams are made.
And so I stayed, my heart at rest,
My soul at peace, my life its best.
The city's call, a distant hum,
For I had found where I belong.
Amidst the trees, the fields, the streams,
I lived a life beyond my dreams.
The choice I made, my heart agreed,
Was the greatest gift I'd ever need.
Here in the village, the world is whole,
A place that nurtures heart and soul.
The city fades, its grip undone,
And in the countryside, I've won.

74. The Promise of a New Dawn

Each morning comes with a burden to bear,
A weight of trials, of thoughts and care.
But cloaked within its gentle glow,
A seed of hope begins to grow.
The first beam pierces the silent sky,
A golden streak where shadows lie.
It travels fast, relentless, true,
To reach your face and awaken you.
This light, a messenger from the sun,
Tells of battles fought and victories won.
It crossed the void in a fleeting breath,
Chasing away the night's cold death.
The dawn unfolds like an artist's dream,
Painting the earth in a radiant gleam.
The sky blushes in hues of red,
As stars retreat, their whispers fled.
Birdsong greets the morning air,
A chorus of life that banishes despair.
The dewdrops cling to blades of green,
Jewels of night in the sunlight seen.
The trees sway gently in the breeze,
Their rustling leaves a symphony of ease.

The rivers glisten, their currents hum,
A melody of the day to come.
Each shadow melts in the morning's glow,
Revealing paths where dreams can grow.
The burdens we carry, heavy and vast,
Are softened by the light that breaks the past.
For every new day, a story is spun,
A chance to start where none's begun.
Though yesterday lingers, etched in time,
Its lessons guide our upward climb.
The past may stay, a shadow near,
A whisper of pain, a fleeting tear.
But look ahead, where futures gleam,
A boundless realm of hope and dream.
The morning beckons, its arms outspread,
To leave behind what's gone, what's dead.
To embrace the now, the moments here,
And venture forth without the fear.
The sun climbs higher, its warmth unfurls,
A golden cloak over the waking world.
The streets awaken, the city hums,
As hearts beat loud like distant drums.
And in the vast expanse of sky,
Clouds drift slowly, soft and high.
They weave a tapestry of grace,
A fleeting canvas time won't replace.
The day is young, the hour still pure,
A treasure chest of dreams unsure.
Its moments wait, like unturned pages,

For us to script through life's vast stages.
So when the light falls on your face,
Know it's traveled a boundless space.
A gift from afar, a cosmic embrace,
To stir your heart with boundless grace.
Let hope ignite within your chest,
A fire that fuels your daily quest.
For though the climb is steep, unknown,
You'll find the strength to stand alone.
Every step you take, each stride,
Is a leap toward the future wide.
The burdens fade, the dreams grow near,
Success takes shape, sharp and clear.
The sun, now high, a blazing crown,
Lights the world and casts doubts down.
Its rays are whispers, soft yet strong,
"Keep moving forward, you belong."
The day moves on, but it's still yours,
A journey through unopened doors.
The night will come, but do not fear,
The dawn will always reappear.
For every burden brings its gift,
A chance to rise, to grow, to lift.
And every dawn, a spark divine,
Reminds you of life's endless design.
So greet the morning, let it stay,
The promise bright of a brand-new day.
In every moment, let hope be born,
For every sunrise holds the morn.

75. The Speck of Eternity

A speck adrift on cosmic seas, a universe confined,
A secret held within its heart, where truths of life unwind.
It floated through the boundless vast, through starlight's endless glow,
An ancient tale of all that is, of all we yearn to know.
From fiery birth in stellar wombs, it shaped the dust of dreams,
A fragment of the infinite, where boundless beauty gleams.
It danced upon the winds of time, a silent, fleeting guest,
A whisper in eternity, a soul that never rests.
It bore the mark of ancient stars, of worlds no eyes could see,
A map of every fleeting life, a song of what could be.
Through tempests wild and quiet shores, it journeyed on its way,
A thread within the tapestry, a dawn in endless day.
Amidst the void where chaos reigns, it wove a tranquil hymn,
A light to guide the lost and frail through corridors grown dim.
In every crevice of its form, creation's secrets lay,
A spark of life, a glint of hope, to chase the night away.
For in the smallest trace of dust, eternity resides,
A witness to the grand design, where endless wonder hides.
It danced among colliding worlds, unyielding in its flight,
A bearer of the cosmos' truth, a fragment of its light.
What lies within a fleeting mote, unseen by mortal eyes?
A universe of boundless dreams, of galaxies and skies.
Its journey mirrors humankind, through joy and bitter strife,
A transient, eternal spark, the miracle of life.

From ashes born, to ashes turned, the cycle never ends,
In every grain, in every star, the cosmos gently bends.
It whispers through the fleeting winds, in silence, it reveals,
The mystery of all we are, the power that it wields.
No moment small, no life too brief, for all is intertwined,
Each speck, a thread in time's great weave, a mark of the divine.
In every heart, a universe, in every soul, a spark,
To light the way through shadowed paths, to guide us through the dark.
So let us cherish every mote, each fleeting breath, each sigh,
For in their depths, eternity reflects the boundless sky.
A speck of dust, a universe, a story yet untold,
A truth that speaks of endless life, in fragile forms of gold.
Through calm and storm, through rise and fall, its purpose still remains,
A speck that carries all of us, through joys and through our pains.
And when we fade, we too shall rest, within its vast embrace,
A part of something infinite, a timeless, sacred space.
A fleeting speck, yet boundless too, a paradox of grace,
A humbling truth that in the dust, the universe finds place.
For in that mote, the cosmos lives, its whispers never cease,
A testament to all that is: creation's masterpiece.

76. The Castle in the Sky

If I could craft a castle high,
Upon the wings that let me fly,
I'd weave its stones from dreams untold,
And mortar it with sunlight's gold.
A fortress borne of hope and air,
Unchained by weight or worldly care,
Its towers kissed by starlit streams,
A haven spun from boundless dreams.
Through azure seas, my castle'd glide,
Where clouds like whispers softly bide,
Above the mountains, vast and grand,
Beyond the touch of mortal hand.
I'd chase the sun across the blue,
Its warmth my guide, its light my clue,
With herons sleek as my escort,
To skies where heaven's thoughts consort.
Through canyons deep and valleys green,
Where Earth's raw beauty reigns serene,
Over rivers twisting, wild and free,
The castle sails—a symphony.
Each morning greets with painted skies,
A burst of light as shadows die,
Each night a calm where stars bestow,
A thousand secrets, soft aglow.

The world below would stop and stare,
At wonders drifting through the air,
A beacon high, where spirits soar,
A call to dream and to explore.
No walls would bind my lofty keep,
Its halls as vast as cosmic deep,
Each room a world, each door a gate,
To paths unknown, to untold fate.
Through storm and gale, it would prevail,
A ship of dreams, an endless sail,
Its course not set, its journey free,
A symbol of infinity.
For castles built on Earthly ground,
Are weighed by stone and roots profound,
But those aloft, on wings of thought,
Are boundless, limitless, unsought.
And as the people gaze in awe,
Their hearts might feel an ancient law,
That life is more than toil and strife,
It's wonder, freedom, endless life.
A lesson whispered on the breeze,
Through castles gliding over seas,
That all we dream, and all we try,
Can build a castle in the sky.
So let us craft with hope's own hand,
A castle none can understand,
Where love and courage dare to fly,
And hearts find solace in the sky.

For in the clouds where dreams ascend,
Our earthly struggles find their end,
A timeless truth, a soul's reply:
Our greatest castle is the sky.

77. The Call of the Patriot

Beyond the lofty mountains high,
Beneath the vast and endless sky,
There lies my home, a sacred place,
Where love awaits with gentle grace.
A maiden fair with beaming face,
Stands steadfast in her warm embrace,
Her arms outstretched, her heart aglow,
A haven where my soul would go.
Yet fate has drawn another line,
My heart beats to a cause divine.
For love more vast than one alone,
For soil and spirit, flesh and bone.
The sun may set, the stars may rise,
But still I guard with watchful eyes.
Upon this land, I hold my ground,
Where duty calls, my soul is bound.
For mine is love not lightly swayed,
Nor to one heart is it conveyed.
My motherland, my sacred soil,
For you I stand, for you I toil.
The enemy lurks, their shadows creep,
Through hills and vales, in silence deep.
Yet undeterred, I hold the line,
For in this fight, my love will shine.

Each stone I guard, each blade of grass,
Holds whispers of the ages past.
Each tree that sways, each river's flow,
Speaks of a land where dreams will grow.
For "Mera Bharat Mahaan," I cry,
With every breath, with every sigh.
Its spirit lives within my veins,
A love that shields, a heart that reigns.
Though far from home my journey wends,
I find my strength where duty bends.
For sacrifice, though steep the cost,
Brings glory found, not honor lost.
The maiden waits, her heart is true,
Yet my first love is ever you.
O Bharat, land of sacred flame,
Your cause transcends all mortal claim.
In fields of gold, in skies of blue,
Your beauty calls, your spirit too.
From ancient stones to future dreams,
Your essence flows through boundless streams.
And though my path is fraught with strife,
I pledge to serve you all my life.
To guard your peace, to hold your light,
Through endless days and darkest night.
For patriot's love knows no retreat,
It walks the fire, it feels the heat.
It bows not down, it does not yield,
It plants its heart upon the field.

So let the mountains hide my home,
Let oceans rise, let tempests roam.
For here I stand, a guardian true,
O Bharat, all I am is you.
And as the dawn ignites the land,
I lift my voice, I raise my hand.
With pride and faith, I humbly state,
"Mera Bharat Mahaan," my fate.
Let others dream of softer days,
Of tranquil nights and gentler ways.
But I will stand, I will defend,
Until the stars in heaven end.
For love of home, of land, of kin,
Is where the truest paths begin.
And in my heart, that truth will reign:
"Mera Bharat Mahaan," again.

78. The Mirror of Belonging

Sometimes, I walk a narrow line,
A place unclear, no fate divine.
I feel adrift, out of my place,
A fleeting shadow, lost in space.
I see the world, its constant flow,
Its scripted paths, its endless show.
And in my heart, a quiet plea,
Why don't I fit? Where should I be?
I bend, I mold, I twist, I change,
To fit a world that feels so strange.
I wear the masks, I play the part,
Suppress the song within my heart.
Yet in this chase, this futile quest,
I lose the self I know the best.
For every shape I try to be,
Still leaves me yearning to be free.
And then a truth, so soft, unfolds,
A whispered thought my mind now holds:
Each soul I see, each face I meet,
Hides the same doubts, the same defeat.
The irony, it starts to gleam,
A twist within this tangled dream:
As I strive hard to mimic grace,
Another longs to take my place.

For what I see as lacking, frail,
Another views as rare and pale.
What I dismiss, a flawed design,
Is treasured gold in others' minds.
The beauty of the self we bear,
Is lost in mirrors cracked with care.
We chase reflections, never whole,
And lose the essence of the soul.
If only I could let me be,
Embrace the truth of being free.
To walk the world with open eyes,
Not seeking masks, but boundless skies.
For no one fits, yet all belong,
In life's grand, chaotic song.
Each note distinct, yet part of all,
Each rise, each fall, a vital call.
The world is vast, yet it refrains,
From crafting copies, bound in chains.
Instead, it gifts uniqueness pure,
A truth no shadow can obscure.
So here I stand, my heart ablaze,
No longer lost in borrowed gaze.
I claim my voice, my story too,
A soul of old, a spark of new.
And if you feel you don't belong,
That who you are is somehow wrong,
Remember this: no star's the same,
Yet all together light the flame.

The journey's not to change your hue,
But shine with all that's truly you.
For in the mirror's fractured frame,
Each shard reflects a burning name.
And as I walk this path once more,
The doubts recede, the heart restores.
I see the self I used to flee,
And find the strength to just be me.
So let us vow to cease the chase,
To honor each unique embrace.
For in our differences, we find,
The endless beauty of mankind.
And thus the world becomes a home,
Where no one ever stands alone.
For every soul, no matter where,
Belongs to life's eternal care.

79. The Dance of Souls

I'd love to hear your voice take flight,
A song that turns the dark to light.
Its melody, a gentle stream,
Awakening my quiet dream.
I'd love to dance without control,
As though I had no weight, no soul.
To spin with joy, unbound, unchained,
Where only freedom's essence reigned.
When I arrive, my heart in hand,
To find no calls, no vague demand,
But yours alone—a voice so true,
A bond that binds me close to you.
Hold my fingers, let them stay,
In your grasp, come what may.
Lean on me, I'll never tire,
I'll carry you through flood and fire.
Together we'll take to the skies,
With winds of trust and hearts that rise.
Side by side, we'll cross the sea,
To realms unknown, where dreams run free.
And on and on, the journey flows,
Through endless days, through highs and lows.
With every step, our bond will grow,
A light eternal, softly aglow.

But when apart, when skies are gray,
And silence fills the passing day,
Know this truth, forever clear:
My essence lingers, always near.
For when you gaze into the glass,
And see your image softly pass,
There I'll be, within your sight,
A shadow cast by love's own light.
You'll find the strength to dance once more,
To twirl, to leap, to touch the floor.
For every move, each gentle spin,
Will speak of all we've held within.
The world may falter, time may flee,
Yet you will always carry me.
Not as a weight, nor fleeting trace,
But as a rhythm time can't erase.
For love's a dance that never dies,
It echoes loud through endless skies.
A force that binds, a truth profound,
A song of life, a sacred sound.
So hold this thought, through joy or pain,
Through loss, through love, through sun, through rain.
You are enough, a soul complete,
With steps unique, with heartbeats sweet.
And as we move through life's great hall,
Together, separate—one and all,
Remember this: you have the role,
To dance as though you had no soul.

For in that dance, the truth will gleam,
A life fulfilled, a vivid dream.
And in that moment, you will find,
The boundless power of heart and mind.

80. When Stars of the Heart Illuminate

When the stars of the heart softly glow,
They hum a tune, a tale they know.
Of times when paths may drift away,
When the light of love seems to stray.
Should you depart, far and wide,
And leave the shores where dreams reside,
If home becomes a fading gleam,
And life feels like a fleeting dream,
When no one calls you their own,
And you wander through lands unknown,
Hold this truth, let it gently stay:
You were never cast away.
For bonds unspoken, deep and vast,
Are stronger than the shadows cast.
Even if the world turns cold,
The warmth of love remains untold.
Speak not of loss, nor pain endured,
For every wound, in time, is cured.
Say instead, with steady grace,
"I've found my light in every space."
When doubts arise, and hope seems thin,
Recall the fire that burns within.

DO WE LIVE, OR JUST EXIST?

A beacon bright, it lights your way,
Through darkest night and weary day.
No step you take is ever lost,
Each one has purpose, no matter the cost.
The stars above, the earth below,
All guide the path your heart must know.
For life's a journey, vast and wide,
A shifting, turning, boundless tide.
And though you roam, and though you stray,
You are never truly far away.
The ties of love, though stretched, remain,
Through joy, through sorrow, through peace, through pain.
And when you pause, when silence reigns,
The hum of those stars still sustains.
So fear not loss, nor distant lands,
Nor the lack of familiar hands.
For every soul, a truth will see:
We are bound by love's eternity.
Say this, when the stars align,
"When I am lost, their light will shine.
Though I wander, though I roam,
I carry within me my eternal home."
And if the world seems vast and cold,
Let your spirit's story unfold.
For hearts that truly love and care,
Are never alone, not here, not there.
So hum the song, let it resound,
Through valleys low, through heights unbound.
And in its echo, softly stay,

TITUS NAZARENE KUJUR

You were never far away.

81. The Poet's Truth

What bond exists between ink and pen,
When heart and mind fail to blend?
For the urge to write dwells in us all,
Yet few dare answer the spirit's call.
To lay bare thoughts that pierce the soul,
To craft with words a story whole,
Is not the work of timid hearts,
But of those who master shadowed arts.
A poet, they say, is one who sees,
Through veils of life, through stormy seas.
Their truth is raw, their voice profound,
In silence vast, their echoes sound.
Not every hand can wield the blade,
That cuts through lies, where fears cascade.
For ink can wound, and ink can heal,
It shapes the world, it makes us feel.
A poet's craft is a rebel's cry,
It shatters chains, it questions why.
It lays the coffin of old despair,
And dares the world to place it there.
With verses bold, they weave a thread,
Between the living and the dead.
They carve out truths from pain's deep core,
And leave us yearning, aching for more.

For words are not mere fleeting streams,
They hold our hopes, our broken dreams.
A poet turns the mundane to art,
And lights a flame in every heart.
But what makes a poet, tell me, friend?
It's not the ink, nor lines they send.
It's the courage to face what others deny,
To smile at grief and never lie.
For poets walk where others fear,
They whisper truths we hate to hear.
And when their words cut sharp and deep,
They rouse the soul from its quiet sleep.
So here's to those who dare to write,
To pen the dark, to sing the light.
For every word, a world is born,
A spark of dawn, a rose from thorn.
Remember this: a poet's role,
Is to unearth the buried soul.
To dress wounds raw, to heal the pain,
To make us feel alive again.
So hail the poet, the fearless one,
Who turns the tides, who greets the sun.
For they, my friend, are rebels pure,
Defining truths that will endure.
And as their ink flows, dark and sure,
They craft a legacy to endure.
For poets are not bound by fate,
They are the voices that create.

82. The Unfinished Dream

Still a dream unfulfilled,
A fleeting vision, yet to build.
It rises in whispers, soft and clear,
A wish, a longing, ever near.
With every breath, with every sigh,
It shimmers beneath the endless sky.
Whether eyes are open, whether they close,
The dream, incomplete, eternally grows.
Each moment it dances, swift and bright,
Fading away with the fall of night.
A vision that vanishes before it's seen,
Like the wind's song, unheard, unseen.
It flutters, a whisper, a silent plea,
Dancing just beyond where we can be.
A promise of something yet to unfold,
A tale untold, a truth still bold.
But it slips, it slides, it fades from sight,
Like stars that vanish with the light.
A dream that beckons, then runs away,
A promise lost at the break of day.
And yet, we chase it, still we yearn,
For something we cannot quite discern.
We grasp at shadows, reach for the sky,

Never seeing it pass us by.
The horizon calls, the future sings,
Of distant lands and brighter wings.
But here we stand, and here we wait,
A dream unfinished, tied by fate.
The world moves on, the day is born,
Yet our hearts ache with the forlorn.
For what is life but an endless chase,
For a dream we cannot embrace?
Sleep, it calls with a gentle sigh,
And still, we wonder why we try.
The night is here, the dream takes flight,
But when dawn breaks, it fades from sight.
"Don't wait for me," it softly says,
"Your morning will find its own way,
The day will come, but not for you,
I am the night, and I am through."
And so we wait, yet still we see,
That the dream, it never lets us be.
For in its silence, we find our quest—
A life half-lived, a soul's unrest.
But in this journey, there lies a truth,
That dreams are not bound by time or youth.
They are the heartbeat of the soul,
The endless longing to feel whole.
So let it go, this fleeting night,
The dream may fade, but in its light,
You'll find a path, a way to go,
For even half-dreamed, life still flows.

And in that flow, you will see,
The dream was never far from thee.
For though incomplete, it's here, it stays,
Guiding your heart through all your days.

83. The Substitute for Hard Work

There's no substitute for hard work,

A truth that runs through time's own murk.

It whispers softly, strong and true,

In every task that we must do.

Through sweat and toil, through endless strife,

Hard work is the architect of life.

It molds the soul, it shapes the mind,

A path to greatness, so defined.

But what if we sought something more,

A substitute to open a door?

To ease the burden, to lessen the load,

Would we still walk the noble road?

We dream of shortcuts, swift and sweet,

A way to make life feel complete.

But in the end, it's always clear,

Hard work's the price for what we hold dear.

There is no magic, no easy key,

To unlock success without the plea.

The sweat of effort, the tears of will,

Are the very things that time distill.

Yet we can create, we can refine,

A new path forward, where stars align.

It's not a shortcut, not an escape,
But a clever way to reshape our fate.
The substitute is not in ease,
But in finding ways that truly please.
It's in innovation, in thought's bold flight,
In seeking truth, in seeking light.
For hard work is the seed we sow,
But how we water, helps it grow.
Creativity, ambition, and grace,
Are the winds that help it embrace.
It's not the task that holds us tight,
But how we see it, how we fight.
The substitute is not to run,
But to make the journey full of fun.
When you work, work with heart and mind,
Not just the body, but the soul intertwined.
The substitute is not to escape,
But to change the world with your own shape.
So let it be known, and let it ring,
There's no substitute for the joy work brings.
For it's not the ease, nor the time you save,
But the satisfaction of what you gave.
Create your own path, let it unfold,
For the substitute for hard work is bold.
It's not in shortcuts, or the fleeting breeze,
But in passion, effort, and the will to seize.
For in the end, when the work is done,
You'll know that you've truly won.
Not because the work was light,

But because you gave it all your might.

84. The Voyage of the Soul

Tonight, we set forth into the unknown,
Just you and me, together, alone.
A torch in your hand, a candle in mine,
Guiding the way through the darkened line.
The path ahead, so long and steep,
A journey through mountains, wild and deep.
We tread with care, yet full of grace,
We know not where, but we embrace the pace.
The night is endless, the sky is bare,
No moon to guide, no stars to share.
Yet in the stillness, a song is sung,
A melody that lives where our hearts are young.
Humming softly, the tune runs deep,
A rhythm that stirs, a promise we keep.
In the sinews of time, etched on the soul,
This melody makes the broken whole.
We know not where this journey leads,
What truth awaits or what heart pleads.
But with each step, we find our way,
For in this darkness, we are meant to stay.
The road may be rough, the night may grow long,
But your presence is where I belong.
For in your company, I find my peace,
A solace so pure, a sweet release.

We do not need to see the end,
For in each moment, we transcend.
The journey's value is in the stride,
Not in the destination we may find.
Together, we weave through shadows and dreams,
With hearts united, or so it seems.
The darkness may hold its endless night,
But we will face it, side by side, in light.
For as long as you are near, my dear,
The road, no matter how unclear,
Becomes a path of endless grace,
A sacred journey, a shared embrace.
So let us walk through this eternal night,
With nothing but faith, hearts burning bright.
For when we face the dark unknown,
We realize we are never alone.
With your hand in mine, through every fear,
The night turns to dawn, and hope draws near.
For the true voyage is not through the sky,
But the bond we share as we journey by.
Together, we shall travel far,
Guided by love, under each star.
In this moment, with you beside me,
I am free, and forever I'll be.

85. The Space to Breathe

At times, the world does not align,
When efforts fail, when plans decline.
The hours stretch, the days fall flat,
And chaos wraps its endless hat.
In the midst of toil, the heart grows tired,
As if all laws of order are expired.
The void within, a silent scream,
An urge to flee, to chase a dream.
But life is not in leaving all,
Not in running from the rise and fall.
For chaos will always find its way,
And trouble will come, come what may.
What we need is not escape,
Not to abandon, nor to reshape.
But a space, so small, so pure,
A breath of calm, a fleeting cure.
Not the vastness of endless skies,
But a moment to close tired eyes.
A space where thoughts can freely flow,
A gentle pause to let life grow.
Go on an adventure, walk the street,
Meet an old friend, feel the heartbeat.
Lie on the grass, with the sun on your face,
Let the clouds move at their own pace.

Open an old book, let the words revive,
A fairy tale that keeps hope alive.
Read those notes, from days of youth,
Find solace in their timeless truth.
The world may not fall into place,
But in that moment, there's grace.
For what is needed is not the fix,
But the simple joys, the tiny tricks.
Those little moments, so sweet and small,
Are the ones that carry us through it all.
They are the fuel for the road ahead,
When the heart is weary and the spirit's dead.
Things may not fall back into line,
The chaos may remain, still entwined.
But those moments, those fragments of peace,
Allow the heart to find release.
Life is not about perfection's quest,
Not about proving we are the best.
It is about breathing, feeling the weight,
And knowing each step is part of fate.
So live it fully, embrace the ride,
Through every storm, with heart open wide.
For in the end, it's not the strife,
But the moments of joy that define your life.
The story is yours, don't try to prove,
Just live each day, let your spirit move.
In the quiet, in the rush, in the space between,
That's where you'll find the life unseen.

86. The Journey of Steps

Step by step, the path unfolds,

A journey new, a story told.

With every footfall, you move ahead,

In pursuit of dreams, where hope is led.

To reach the stars, to touch the sky,

You must take the steps, no question why.

The urge to begin, to take the chance,

Will lead you to that distant dance.

Each step a promise, a choice you make,

A challenge faced, a risk you take.

The mind that creates, the heart that dares,

Will push you forward, beyond all fears.

Count the steps, one by one,

As the race is fought, but never won.

For each step taken is a victory near,

A testament to courage, to hold dear.

The longer the stride, the further you fly,

With each passing moment, you touch the sky.

Your success is built, not on luck or fate,

But on the steps you take, and never wait.

Decisions shape your path ahead,

The dreams you chase, the words you've said.

Challenges arise, but they'll fall away,

When you keep moving forward, day by day.

Creativity sparks within your mind,
A light that guides, so bold, so kind.
Motivation lies within your heart,
A force that pushes you to start.
A team to lead, a vision clear,
Every step strengthens what you hold dear.
For every step you take with pride,
Leads you closer to the other side.
Along the way, don't walk alone,
Share your thoughts, let your heart be shown.
Communicate, connect, and share,
For the journey's richer when you care.
Appreciate the moments, big and small,
For they are the stepping stones to it all.
Delve into the unknown, embrace the ride,
With open arms, let curiosity guide.
There's no mystery to uncover, no wall too tall,
Just keep moving forward, answering the call.
Let the adventure be your guiding star,
And celebrate the progress, no matter how far.
At the end of the day, with joy, you'll say,
That the journey was worth it, in every way.
For you moved, you learned, you led with might,
And in the end, you'll know you did it right.
So take your steps, keep moving through,
For the world awaits, and it's waiting for you.
In each stride, in each breath, in every cheer,
The adventure calls—so step forward, my dear.

87. The Time Weaver's Loom

In a shadowed ruin where whispers stay,
She sat at her loom, spinning night from day.
Her hands, though frail, moved with timeless grace,
An ageless beauty on her ancient face.
The threads she pulled were like rivers that glide,
Flowing through fingers, too vast to hide.
Cobwebs hung thick, a shroud of despair,
Yet the cloak she wove glimmered bright and rare.
Each strand a hue, from gray to gold,
Telling the stories of lives untold.
Patterns of rainbows and shadows deep,
Dreams that awaken, or tears that seep.
I stepped with caution, drawn by the art,
Each stitch a tale, each color a heart.
Her eyes met mine, like a frozen stream,
And her cruel smile broke my dream.
"Why do you come to my woven tide?
Do you seek your fate, or a truth denied?"
Her voice was sharp, like a knife through the air,
Her question lingered, heavy and bare.
"Who are you?" I asked, my courage thin,
Her laugh echoed, a chilling din.
"I am the Time Weaver," she said with pride,
"Naerthara, mistress of life's great tide.

With my loom, I spin the grand design,
Dull or vibrant, it is all divine.
Before a child draws their first sweet breath,
I weave the tale of their life—and death.
The joy they'll feel, the trials they'll face,
The love they'll find, their fall from grace.
No thread escapes, no pattern breaks,
For what I weave, the world partakes."
Her words sank deep, like anchors to ground,
In her hands, the fate of all was bound.
"Why weave sorrow?" I dared to say,
"Why not let the threads dance and play?"
Her smile returned, as sharp as stone,
"Without the dark, the light's unknown.
Each thread of grief, each strand of woe,
Teaches the soul how to truly grow.
The dullest strands hold wisdom's weight,
The brightest hues may herald fate.
Life is a tapestry, both cruel and kind,
Its beauty lies in what you find."
I watched her weave, her hands so sure,
Her art both haunting and obscure.
A child's first laugh, a widow's cry,
All were woven as time slipped by.
"What of my thread?" I asked with dread,
"What lies before me? What lies ahead?"
She paused, her needle hanging midair,
Her piercing gaze a frozen glare.

"Your thread is yours, though I set its course,
You hold the reins, you steer the horse.
Though I decide when your life will cease,
How you live it is your own release.
Will you weave love into the loom?
Or let despair foretell your doom?
The cloak I spin may guide your way,
But you choose what colours to display."
Her words like echoes haunted my mind,
A truth so harsh, yet deeply kind.
The loom kept moving, her rhythm stayed,
As the cloak stretched longer, arrayed and swayed.
"Go now," she said, her voice like frost,
"Your questions linger, but time is lost.
I weave for the world, for the lives to come,
While you must journey to your own drum."
I turned to leave, her figure so still,
Her weaving eternal, her boundless will.
The ruin behind me, the lesson clear,
In her loom, all futures appear.
Naerthara, the weaver of time's great thread,
Holds our beginnings, and when we're dead.
But in between, the choice is ours,
To bloom like roses, or wilt like flowers.

88. My Gypsy Girl

I gaze at you with silent eyes,
A dream you are, beneath these skies.
A soul so free, yet far away,
A gypsy heart that cannot stay.
I would love to keep you near,
To chase away this lonesome fear.
But you wander, roads untamed,
A fire unbound, a soul unnamed.
You tread where stars dare not descend,
And seek horizons without an end.
I wait in shadows, still and small,
Hoping one day you'll heed my call.
Your spirit dances with the breeze,
Through golden fields and ancient seas.
Yet here I stand, a steady flame,
Unmoving, though the winds may claim.
Oh, to hold your hand just once,
To whisper words my heart confronts.
But you, an eagle in the sky,
Will never pause to wonder why.
You soar above, the earth a blur,
Each height a song, each wind a stir.
While I remain, my roots grow deep,
A silent vigil, a love to keep.

One day, perhaps, the winds will tire,
And quench the blaze of your desire.
You'll seek a hearth, a steady shore,
A place where you'll wander no more.
When that day comes, I'll still be here,
Through seasons lost and countless years.
A home for you, as still as stone,
For only with you, am I truly home.
And though your journey calls you now,
With restless wings and furrowed brow,
I know the earth will call you back,
To mend the trail of all you lack.
So fly, my love, with boundless grace,
Discover every unknown place.
For when the skies no longer please,
I'll hold your heart with tender ease.
This waiting is not born of pain,
But of a love that will remain.
A quiet strength, a steadfast plea,
That one day you'll come home to me.
And if you never choose to stay,
I'll bless your path, your chosen way.
For love is not a chain or tether,
It's wings that journey storms together.
So carry my heart where'er you go,
Through sunlit fields or peaks of snow.
And when the world feels cold and blue,
Know there is a home, waiting for you.

Until that day, I'll light the flame,
And whisper softly, your cherished name.
For love like mine cannot deny,
An eagle soaring in the sky.

89. A Love Beyond Reason

However hard I try to lose you, it will never suffice,
For a part of you lingers, silent and precise.
Like grains of sand slipping through my grasping hand,
Yet clinging softly, a memory unmanned.
Across the road, where the café's hum resides,
You step with grace as the morning sun collides.
Your satin red dress, a blazing celestial flame,
A beauty so vivid, it whispers your name.
I stand at the bus stop, a paper in my clutch,
Yet my eyes betray me, seeking your touch.
The headlines blur into meaningless scrawl,
For love has consumed me, its madness my all.
Around me, the world continues its haste,
Feet rushing, time flowing, moments displaced.
The old cobbler mends a shoe with care,
While a child cries out for a balloon in despair.
The aroma of coffee drifts with the breeze,
A melody of chatter under the trees.
Clinking cups and laughter harmonize,
As sunlight dances in strangers' eyes.
A man in a suit checks his silver watch,
Impatience writ clear as he adjusts his botch.
A couple strolls by, hands tightly entwined,
Their silent communion a solace defined.

Yet I stand still, a statue of thought,
Bound by a love that sanity forgot.
Your reflection in the cafe window glows,
A beacon of warmth in my life's endless prose.
"She's moved on," the whispers say,
"New friends, new paths, a brighter day."
But what do they know of love's quiet scream,
Of holding on to the remnants of a dream?
The world paints me mad, a fool in despair,
For staring too long, for daring to care.
But what is love if not a divine madness,
A blissful torment, a sweet sadness?
I see the barista pour a frothy brew,
Steam rising like hopes, ephemeral and new.
The waiter smiles as he clears a plate,
Each gesture imbued with its own quiet fate.
The bus rumbles in, its brakes a shrill call,
Yet I remain rooted, indifferent to all.
Passengers board, their stories unseen,
While I gaze at you, my eternal queen.
The pigeons coo and flutter their wings,
Seeking crumbs in life's simple things.
A street musician plucks his guitar,
His melody drifting like dreams afar.
Your laughter spills like a stream of light,
Filling the cafe with echoes bright.
I wonder, do you notice my gaze?
Or am I a shadow in love's endless maze?

Let the world call me mad, I embrace the refrain,
For love without madness is hollow and vain.
To love is to lose, yet find yourself anew,
In the depths of longing, the chaos of you.
The day wanes on, the sun begins to set,
Casting hues of amber, a silhouette.
You rise, you leave, a fleeting trace,
And I, a dreamer, remain in this space.
The bus stop, the cafe, the bustling street,
All fade away where memories meet.
For love is eternal, a timeless refrain,
A madness that soothes, a sweet, gentle pain.
And so I stand, my heart a flame,
A witness to love's relentless claim.
The world may move, but I stay here,
Forever bound by a love sincere.

90. The Prince and the Hidden Truth

In England's land, where myths still flow,
Where meadows bloom and rivers glow,
A tale was told through whispers old,
Of a touchstone rare that turned lead to gold.
By Avonlea's gentle, winding stream,
Where waters danced and willows dream,
The story spread like morning dew,
Of a stone whose magic none yet knew.
"A fable," scoffed the wise and proud,
"A dream for fools, a tale too loud."
But a young prince, bold, with heart aflame,
Chose to chase this legend's claim.
With buckle of lead clasped at his waist,
He stepped forth with eager haste.
The morning sun in splendor rose,
Painting fields in golden glows.
The forest called with pine-sweet air,
Its leaves a choir, its whispers rare.
Birds flitted high in a sapphire sky,
And bees hummed soft as time slipped by.
Stone by stone, his hands would glean,
Touching each to the buckle's sheen.

With hopeful heart, he tested all,
Yet none transformed, no gold would call.
Through brambles thick and fern-lined trails,
By brooks that sang their merry tales,
The prince pressed on with boundless glee,
For hope still danced like the wildwood tree.
By Avonlea's banks, where waters sighed,
And reeds swayed gently with the tide,
He knelt to touch each river stone,
Yet felt no magic in their tone.
Noon's bright eye burned through the wood,
His spirit dimmed, though he understood:
"A fool, perhaps, to seek the grand,
In simple stones within my hand."
He lingered yet, though faith grew thin,
Picking stones with a weary grin.
Throwing them far, he ceased to care,
The legend seemed a hollow dare.
The day grew old, the shadows long,
The forest hummed a twilight song.
And so, the prince, tired and spent,
To the castle gates his journey bent.
Within his chamber's velvet glow,
He cast his belt to the bed below.
But as it landed with a clang,
A golden light from the buckle sprang!
He froze in awe, his breath a sigh,
The dull lead gone, gold gleamed nearby.
Bewildered now, he ran with haste,

To Avonlea's shores, the stones retraced.
A candle flickered in trembling hand,
He searched once more the river's strand.
Stone by stone, he touched anew,
But the magic stone eluded view.
For the touchstone hid in plain disguise,
As common as clouds in autumn skies.
No mark to show, no hue to tell,
It blended in the forest's spell.
And so, the prince, though young and wise,
Learned a truth beneath the skies:
The rarest treasures, the truest gold,
Are often plain and shy to behold.
How oft we judge by outward grace,
By wealth or charm, or a comely face.
Yet hidden in the humblest guise,
A touchstone dwells, unseen by eyes.
Avonlea murmured its ageless song,
As the prince reflected all night long.
"The stone was there, yet I was blind,
Its worth concealed, its truth confined.
So too with people, plain and small,
Who hold within a gift for all.
The heart, a gold no eyes can see,
A wealth that shapes eternity."
Thus ends the tale of lead and stone,
Of magic sought and wisdom grown.
May we all, like the prince, recall,
That hidden treasures outshine them all.

91. Dreams Worth Living

Madagascar's waters, so vivid, so clear,
I'd swim with the creatures that dwell without fear.
The coral's kaleidoscope, vibrant and true,
A world full of colours, an infinite hue.
Then hiking the canyons of Arizona's lands,
Through red rock cathedrals shaped by time's hands.
The desert whispers its ancient refrain,
A hymn of endurance through wind and through rain.
Las Vegas would sparkle, a desert of light,
Where dreams are gambled through the shimmering night.
The cards, the dice, the wheel that spins,
A palace of chances where fortune begins.
A cowboy I'd be, with a hat and a grin,
Riding the plains where the wild winds spin.
The sunset would paint the horizon with fire,
A life unrestrained, free of desire.
James Bond I would play, suave and refined,
A spy of intrigue with a razor-sharp mind.
The glamour, the danger, the thrill of the chase,
A tuxedo-clad hero with elegance and grace.
And Broadway would beckon with lights that gleam,
A stage where I'd dance, a star in the stream.
My name in bold letters, a marquee aglow,
The audience cheering, a world they'd bestow.
On the cover of Vogue, my face would appear,
A fashion icon the world would revere.
Styled to perfection, with flair and finesse,
A symbol of dreams in a radiant dress.

But alas, reality keeps me confined,
A world of work and the daily grind.
Yet in my mind, I can journey afar,
To places where dreams are brighter than stars.
For dreaming costs neither a dime nor a penny,
A treasure so vast, not possessed by many.
In my heart, these adventures are perfectly true,
A fantasy world where the soul can renew.
So here I shall dwell, in my castles of air,
Climbing each peak, with the wind in my hair.
Dancing through jungles, sailing the seas,
Living the life of my wildest dreams.
Dreams worth living, they carry no chain,
Through them, I escape from life's mundane.
The world is my canvas, painted anew,
And in this vast world, all dreams come true.

92. The Quiet of a Powerless Day

The power was out, and silence took reign,
No hum of machines, no flicker of flame.
The afternoon lay warm, still as a stone,
And a bead of sweat on my brow shone.
No internet whispers to fill up the void,
No worldly connection to keep me employed.
I sought a siesta to escape the heat,
But slumber had wandered far from my reach.
I opened the cupboard, its hinges a sigh,
Ran fingers through spines where stories reside.
Agatha Christie, her mysteries clear,
Robert Ludlum's intrigue, once held me near.
Naomi Starkey, her tales of the soul,
Isaac Asimov's visions, so vivid, so whole.
Yet all were familiar, their pages worn thin,
Each line, each twist, engraved deep within.
Bereft of new journeys, I turned to my past,
Pulled out old diaries, their memories amassed.
I read aloud, though no ear was near,
My voice the only sound I could hear.
Then sketches I drew with hands unsure,
But my mind lacked the spark it once ensured.

The pencil faltered, the paper lay bare,
Imagination asleep, I could not care.
So I set it aside, left the house behind,
Stepped into a world both vast and confined.
Through the deserted lane, my feet found their way,
To fields where the paddy in emerald lay.
The rice stalks swayed in a gentle breeze,
A sea of green under skies at ease.
The clouds drifted softly, painted in white,
Shaped like dreams in the afternoon light.
Birds flew by in a harmonious stream,
Wings slicing the air in a choreographed dream.
Their songs filled the air with a tranquil sound,
A symphony born where peace abounds.
I sat on the earth, warm under my palm,
And let the surroundings restore my calm.
The fields whispered stories of life and of toil,
Of farmers who nurture this sacred soil.
The wind carried scents of blossoms nearby,
Of jasmine and earth, of grass newly dry.
Each breath I inhaled was rich, profound,
A healing elixir the world had unwound.
The sky, a vast canvas, stretched endlessly,
A reminder of life's sheer simplicity.
I watched as the sun cast a golden hue,
Transforming the fields into a sacred view.
Time felt still, yet fleeting, as I sat,
In nature's embrace, where my thoughts unpacked.
The paddy, the breeze, the birds, and the sun,

Became my companions till the day was done.
I pondered the moments that life often hides,
In the quiet of fields where peace resides.
No need for novels or sketches or screens,
The world itself is the grandest of dreams.
For even in silence, adventure is near,
In the rustle of leaves, in the songs we hear.
In the vastness of skies, in clouds that drift,
Life offers us treasures, a timeless gift.
As I walked back home through the evening glow,
The warmth of the earth had begun to show,
That even a powerless day holds its charms,
When you lean on nature's welcoming arms.
So now when the power fails and silence calls,
I embrace the stillness, the absence of walls.
For the world is alive with wonders untold,
In its quiet, we find treasures of gold.

93. The Story of Us

I long to share a million secrets,
But then, they wouldn't be secrets anymore.
They would fade like whispers on the wind,
Leaving silence where wonder once soared.
I dream to tiptoe into your world,
While moonlight guards your quiet rest.
To trace the edges of your dreams,
And weave myself where you are blessed.
To play a guitar, soft and low,
While your spirit drifts in twilight's glow.
Each note a promise, a tender vow,
To love you more than time allows.
For you, I'd wait through endless nights,
Through shifting stars and fading lights.
I'd lose it all, give everything true,
For the simple joy of loving you.
Be by my side, through life's vast song,
Walk with me, where we both belong.
Till our hair turns silver, our hands grow old,
Till the earth grows still, and the tales are told.
And when we rest, beneath the sky,
Let the world remember the reasons why.
That love like ours, so deeply tied,
Can outlast time, can never die.

Be my sunshine when the heavens weep,
The warmth that wakes me from my sleep.
Be my shade when the sun burns high,
The solace beneath the endless sky.
Come dance with me where no one sees,
Let laughter flow like the gentle breeze.
For in your joy, my soul takes flight,
A boundless flame in the darkest night.
Love me as though the world stood still,
As if no one else ever will.
Let me be the one you trust,
Your story of love, your epic, your must.
Be my muse, my sacred song,
The place my heart has searched so long.
With you, each moment feels complete,
A tapestry where love and life meet.
Teach me courage when fear takes hold,
Guide my steps when the night grows cold.
Be my anchor in the storm's fierce call,
My steady hand when I might fall.
And if I falter, lend me grace,
With your love, I'll find my place.
Together, we'll stand through every tide,
With hearts as one, forever tied.
Let's build a world of wonder and light,
Where hope remains through the longest night.
With every trial, we'll find new ways,
To let love bloom in endless days.

Be the star that lights my sky,
The dream that never says goodbye.
In every moment, near or far,
You are my home, my guiding star.
If storms may come, if skies may break,
Your love's the shield I'll always take.
And in the stillness, when all seems gone,
Your warmth remains, my endless dawn.
For you, my love, I'll give my all,
Through rise and fall, through great and small.
You are the reason my soul takes flight,
The beacon shining through the night.
So come, my love, and walk with me,
Let's carve our path through destiny.
Be my story, my life, my art,
And I'll hold you forever in my heart.
When time has passed, when years are done,
We'll rest together, our journey won.
And in the echoes of life's refrain,
Our love will rise, forever again.

94. Never Say Goodbye

Never say goodbye, even if you must depart,
For your essence lingers deep within my heart.
Even when distance keeps you far from me,
I'll hold your memory, as vast as the sea.
I'll wait for you, till the end of all days,
Through life's shifting tides, its mysterious ways.
While you're gone, I'll write with a trembling hand,
Our sweet memories, like castles in the sand.
I'll visit the places where we once strolled,
The park where the sun painted stories untold.
The rustling leaves whispered our names in delight,
Under the canopy of stars in the tranquil night.
I'll walk the shore where the waves kissed our feet,
The sea's endless hymn, so serene, so sweet.
The salty breeze will carry your laughter anew,
Echoing softly, as if calling out to you.
The café where time seemed to slip away,
Where words and silence wove their ballet.
I'll sit by the window, your favorite chair,
Imagining you still lingering there.
In bookstores, I'll linger among dusty tomes,
Seeking your smile in their whispered tones.
In museums, I'll trace the art we admired,
Feeling the warmth of a love never tired.

I'll visit theaters, dimmed with their glow,
Where stories unfolded, and time moved slow.
Each act will remind me of our shared gaze,
A moment frozen in love's endless maze.
At home, I'll gather our photographs near,
Each one a story, a memory dear.
I'll make a collage and hang it with care,
A shrine to the love we promised to share.
When it rains, I'll sit by the windowpane,
Counting droplets like whispers of your name.
Each gleam a reminder of jokes we told,
Laughter immortal, worth more than gold.
As the sun sets and the world turns gray,
I'll look to the sky as night steals the day.
The stars will shine, scattered and bright,
A puzzle of dreams in the vast quiet night.
I'll join those stars, tracing shapes we knew,
Connecting them softly, from me to you.
Knowing somewhere, under this same sky,
You watch them too, as moments pass by.
In every place, your shadow will stay,
A presence eternal, though you're far away.
The sea, the café, the park in the light—
Each holds a fragment of our shared delight.
Even in solitude, you're never gone,
Your love, a melody I dwell upon.
It fills the spaces where silence resides,
A song of forever, where hope abides.

Though time may stretch, though miles may grow,
The bond we share will continue to glow.
For love, my dear, is a tether divine,
Unbroken by distance, unmeasured by time.
When the winds rise and the seasons change,
When the world feels vast and hearts estrange,
I'll still hold fast to the truth I've known—
With you, I am never truly alone.
So never say goodbye, not even in jest,
For our love transcends life's fleeting quest.
In rain, in stars, in places we've been,
I'll find you again, and again, and again.
Even when fate pulls us far apart,
I'll carry your laughter within my heart.
So long as the sky and earth remain,
I'll cherish this love through joy and pain.
Come back someday, but until then,
I'll dream of the moment we meet again.
For love is eternal, and hearts do know,
Never say goodbye, for I'll never let go.

95. The Measure of a Life

You lived a life with breath so fierce,
Yet never truly lived, it appears.
In passion's grasp, your heart did yearn,
Yet light of dawn, your eyes could not discern.
You gathered treasures, wealth untold,
In vaults of greed, your soul was sold.
Yet riches vast could not fulfill,
The hollow echo of your will.
I, who sold myself for mere pennies and stones,
Conquered the world, though stripped to bones.
In humble stride, I found my grace,
While you lost yours in a ceaseless chase.
Your spirit once soared, unchained, unbound,
But fell to earth, with shackles crowned.
What tethered you, what clipped your wings?
The weight of desires and fleeting things.
I bled for dreams, I starved for art,
Yet fed the hunger within my heart.
While you, who fed on life's grand feast,
Found no solace, no inner peace.
What use is the mansion, the glittering gold,
When warmth of love slips through the hold?
What worth is the power, the fleeting fame,
When none remember your heart, your name?

You chased the mirage, the shining star,
And lost yourself in lands afar.
I walked the path of toil and strife,
Yet found the essence of true life.
You feared the fall, you feared the pain,
But without rain, what blooms remain?
I fell, I broke, yet I arose,
And found my strength in life's harsh throes.
You sought to rule, to reign, to thrive,
But lost the wisdom to feel alive.
I gave away what little I had,
And gained the joy that made me glad.
Oh, friend, the truth is hard to see:
To live is not to merely be.
It's in the giving, the breaking, the mending,
The moments fleeting, yet unending.
You lived for gain, for power, for pride,
But in the mirror, could you confide?
That in your quest for life's bright gleam,
You lost the beauty of the dream.
While I, who wandered paths unknown,
Found treasures carved in hearts, not stone.
My poverty was wealth untold,
A richness neither bought nor sold.
The world you built with mighty hands,
Now crumbles into shifting sands.
Yet the love I shared, the lives I touched,
Remain eternal, uncorrupt.

So, when the final curtain falls,
And silence echoes through life's halls,
It's not in wealth, nor in acclaim,
But in the legacy of love we name.
Thus, I leave you this thought to keep:
Life's essence blooms where hearts do weep.
And though I lived a pauper's song,
In death, I've found where I belong.

96. When Storms Met and Time Stood Still

When storms embraced, folding into one,
None knew when their fury was done.
When the sky parted ways with the land below,
None could tell how far they'd let go.
In the shadowed cradle of closed eyes,
The light withdrew, bound by silent ties.
The lamp of the heart, once burning bright,
Succumbed to darkness, consumed by night.
Even in daylight, shadows reigned,
A chill lingered where warmth once remained.
We journeyed far, beyond the bounds of time,
Lost in a maze with no path to climb.
The way back home, a forgotten thread,
Woven into the labyrinth we tread.
Who now would wait by the fading shore,
When we betray ourselves, forevermore?
In the mirror of years, faces fade,
Dreams dissolve, and promises cascade.
We became exiles in our own gaze,
Seeking ourselves through endless haze.
When did the stars lose their silver glow?
When did the rivers forget to flow?

Boundless oceans in our hearts grew dry,
Yet none could say how or why.
The storms within, they raged so fierce,
Tearing through the walls they pierced.
But silence followed, haunting and deep,
A lullaby for the lost who couldn't weep.
We searched the heavens for signs of grace,
Yet found only echoes in empty space.
Time, a thief, stole our youth away,
And left us longing for yesterday.
We carved our names on stones of regret,
Memories etched we can't forget.
Yet even as we reached for the past,
We knew such moments would never last.
Now here we stand, alone and apart,
Carrying shadows within our heart.
The roads we walked are lost to sight,
Consumed by the veil of endless night.
Would someone wait, where we belong?
Or is the truth we've waited too long?
The ones we were are ghosts in the rain,
Wandering souls, bound by pain.
In this silent storm, we came to find,
A reflection of the storms inside.
We became strangers to the ones we knew,
And strangers, too, to the lives we drew.
If ever a dawn could break this chain,
And bring back love through all the pain,
Perhaps the storms would finally cease,

And leave behind the gift of peace.
Yet until then, we drift and roam,
Lost in ourselves, without a home.
Betrayed by the wait, by our own despair,
Chasing shadows that vanish in air.
For the storms have merged, time won't restart,
And we are lost to our own heart.

97. Lost to Myself

I do not know when I lost my way,
When the mirror turned from me, kept me at bay.
In foreign streets, a stranger I became,
An echo of myself, unknown by name.
Companions once walked these roads with me,
Yet behind their masks, no truth I see.
Their faces speak, but their hearts are still,
And I cannot bridge the growing rift of will.
Nights and days blurred into one,
Chasing shadows of what I'd become.
The glass no longer shows my face,
Even its depths have erased my trace.
A friend once said, "The world's a stage,"
But this play unfolds in a barren cage.
Beneath the canopy of borrowed smiles,
I wander through empty miles.
The colours of the sun have faded away,
Its warmth abandoned the edge of the day.
Now even in darkness, shadows creep,
Haunted by whispers that rob my sleep.
A strange city hums, its pulse unknown,
Among countless people, I walk alone.
They pass me by, their voices blurred,
None stop to speak a tender word.

Neighbors line the streets in endless rows,
But none can touch the ache that grows.
Familiar faces, distant and cold,
A tapestry of stories that remain untold.
The world has marched ahead in time,
Yet the rhythm feels like an old rhyme.
Roads stretch out in lifeless grace,
Their endings lost in an endless race.
Home lies somewhere, I've been told,
But its warmth has vanished; the hearth is cold.
What once was mine has turned askew,
A house of memories long overdue.
In the silence, the wind gently sings,
A hymn of sorrow its whispers bring.
The stars blink down, weary and faint,
Their light dimmed by the weight of complaint.
Even the moon hides behind its veil,
Ashamed of this world's mournful tale.
Its glow, a ghost of what it once gave,
Illuminates paths to no one's grave.
I've wandered through moments, lost in thought,
Searching for meaning, but meaning is not.
The earth beneath feels foreign, estranged,
Its touch familiar but somehow changed.
Yet in this stillness, a seed takes root,
Born from despair, it bears its fruit.
For though I walk this lonely tide,
The spark of hope cannot subside.

Perhaps one day, when the mask is torn,
When dawn arrives with a sun reborn,
I'll find my way through the shadows deep,
And wake to a world where love can seep.
But until then, I drift and roam,
A soul untethered, far from home.
The roads remain tied to weary feet,
Yet they whisper secrets I long to meet.
Though strangers pass and years unfold,
My story remains for the stars to hold.
For even in silence, I'm learning to see,
That in losing myself, I am setting me free.

98. The Journey Beyond the Shores

On the shores, boats too sink in their time,
Reaching the shore, they weep for their climb.
Before the flowers bloom, they fade away,
Before the dawn breaks, they lose their way.
Nights passed in silence, without a dream,
Living without hope, just drifting downstream.
We sought destinations that we never found,
And lost our breath before the path could resound.
I think of moving forward, with hope in hand,
But the broken heart whispers, "Take a stand."
"Pause for a while," it says with gentle plea,
"There's no need to rush, there's no place to be."
A journey without a companion feels so long,
Even with the destination, something feels wrong.
Victory may come, but sorrow will follow,
A fable of joy, wrapped in the hollow.
The winds are cold, the road seems so far,
I walk, but the path is marked by scars.
The world is quiet, yet restless inside,
The more I chase, the more I hide.
My dreams were like stars, distant and bright,
But the more I reached, the further from sight.

In the depths of my heart, I long for a light,
But it flickers faintly, as day turns to night.
Before I could speak, the words turned to dust,
Before I could trust, I lost my trust.
I ask the sky, "Why must we fall?"
But no answer comes, only silence calls.
The heart, broken, tells me to wait,
"Patience, dear soul, it's not too late."
A journey alone may break the spirit,
But the destination's not always worth the merit.
What is a journey if you walk alone?
What is a destination if you reach it unknown?
Every step we take, a story we write,
But sometimes we lose ourselves in the fight.
I think of the road that once felt so clear,
Now lost in the fog, drowned by fear.
I've climbed the mountains, crossed the seas,
But in the end, what do I truly seize?
In the silence, the heart speaks loud,
We are just souls in a restless crowd.
Seeking the world, but losing the peace,
Running from sorrow, yet it doesn't cease.
Would a companion make the path less long?
Would the heart heal if it weren't so strong?
For even after winning, the loss remains,
A story of joy, but wrapped in pains.
So I pause for a moment, and let the wind blow,
I don't know where it'll take me, but I'll go slow.
For in this silence, I learn to see,

That sometimes the journey is all there is to be.
And maybe someday, when the road does end,
I'll understand why it's broken to mend.
For each step taken, each tear shed,
Leads to the peace where I'll rest my head.

99. Whispers in the Cracks

In shadows cast by walls that crack,
Whispers linger, yearning to unpack.
Echoes of sighs in silence dwell,
A story untold, too broken to tell.
Once, perhaps, in a fleeting age,
A seeker left behind this cage.
Dreams of joy, he chased afar,
Guided only by a distant star.
He left these walls to search for gold,
To find a warmth that couldn't grow cold.
But treasures sought on foreign shores
Often leave behind unseen wars.
Far away in a crowd so grand,
He builds his castle on shifting sand.
Among strangers, he wears a smile,
Yet his heart is heavy all the while.
For joy that blooms on borrowed ground
Is like a bird in a cage unbound.
It flits, it flies, but doesn't stay,
Leaving shadows in its play.
And so, one day, as stars descend,
And borrowed lights begin to end,
The seeker feels an aching call,
A pull toward the crumbled wall.

With weary feet and hollow gaze,
He treads the path of ancient days.
Back to the cracks, the whispers' keep,
To the walls that never learned to sleep.
He finds the ruins of his past,
The shadows that forever last.
And in the cracks where whispers lie,
He learns the truth he can't deny.
Happiness, he learns, was never far,
Not in gold, nor in the stars.
It breathed within these walls of stone,
It thrived in love he had disowned.
He sits amidst the echoes' hum,
Singing softly, "I've returned home."
For joy, he sees, is not a prize,
But a mirror reflecting familiar skies.
The cracks, they whisper truths profound,
That love is found where roots are bound.
No wealth, no crowd, no fleeting glee
Can anchor a heart that's lost at sea.
So here he stays, in shadows deep,
Among the walls where sorrows weep.
But now he knows, these whispers hold
A wealth far greater than gems or gold.
Let the world chase fleeting highs,
Let it covet its hollow skies.
For the heart finds peace, the soul its tune,
Not in the sun, but beneath the moon.

A lesson born of time and pain,
That loss is sometimes the truest gain.
For joy, it seems, was home all along,
Humming softly its eternal song.

• 283 •

100. The Lessons of Life

Who is a teacher, wise and true?
Not just the one in halls we knew,
But one who speaks in silence, clear,
Through nature's pulse, both far and near.
Beneath the sun, where shadows blend,
A bird in flight becomes a friend.
Its wings, a map of fearless skies,
Inspire dreams that dare to rise.
The forest whispers through its leaves,
In rustling tones, the heart believes.
An ant that toils, though small and frail,
Teaches grit when hardships prevail.
A roaring river, wild and wide,
Flows with truth and sheds its pride.
It bends to rocks, yet finds its way,
A lesson etched in every spray.
The mountain peak, austere and cold,
Speaks of patience, brave and bold.
Its jagged cliffs, where storms collide,
Reveal the strength of what's inside.
If someone pushes, and you fall,
The earth will teach you to stand tall.
Its steady arms embrace the weight,
To rise again, it says, is fate.

And when a hand lifts you with care,
A warmth ignites, beyond compare.
Friendship blooms, a sacred art,
A tether strong, a healing heart.
But should betrayal cut you deep,
And shadows in your spirit creep,
The lesson comes with sharpened hue,
Of trust's frail thread, both false and true.
To forgive, though pain may linger long,
Is to show the weak that you are strong.
To forget, a path not all may tread,
But some things must be left unsaid.
The world's a teacher, vast and wise,
Its classroom spans the endless skies.
Its chalk, the stars, its board, the seas,
Its lessons whispered through the breeze.
In joy, in sorrow, in despair,
The greatest truths are everywhere.
So open wide your heart, your mind,
And leave no trace of fear behind.
For life itself will always teach,
In every soul, it strives to reach.
The journey's long, the lessons clear,
With every step, the truth grows near.

101. When Death Comes to Me

When death will come, I shall not hide,
I'll wait for him with quiet pride.
My bags are packed, my soul prepared,
No fear, no sorrow will be shared.
He won't search, for he knows well,
The place I live, where I dwell.
Through moonlit paths or sunlit air,
His steps will find me waiting there.
He'll come not as a thief in the night,
But as an old friend, cloaked in light.
His hood may shadow his ancient face,
Yet his presence holds a calming grace.
The day will soften, the winds will sigh,
Clouds will scatter, the birds will fly.
The earth will hum a gentle tune,
As stars awaken beneath the moon.
Death's hand will reach, steady and kind,
No weight of sorrow will I find.
His staff will guide, his step serene,
A bridge to where life feels unseen.
He'll lead me past the toil and care,
To a realm where skies are always fair.

Where sunsets rest, but never fade,
And peace resides in every glade.
No hunger there, no need to strive,
Just endless calm, forever alive.
The golden fields, the rivers wide,
Will soothe the soul, no tears to hide.
By a fire's glow, I'll take my seat,
The warmth of eternity at my feet.
A pipe in hand, my heart at ease,
Watching the birds dance on the breeze.
Their wings will paint the boundless sky,
Their songs will lift, both low and high.
In that eternal, endless land,
I'll watch and dream, pipe in hand.
No burdens here, no weight to bear,
Just gentle whispers in the air.
The world will fade, but not in pain,
For death will guide me home again.
So when he comes, I'll smile and say,
"Old friend, I've waited for this day."
With steady steps, I'll walk beside,
His quiet staff, my faithful guide.
And though his hood may shade his face,
I'll feel his warmth, his soft embrace.
For death's not cruel, as some may fear,
But a bridge to home, forever near.

102. The Passing Tides of Friendship

When you leave, what will I do?
The echoes of your laughter will haunt me through.
Shadows of memories will dance on my wall,
As the silence deepens in the empty hall.
Perhaps I'll search for an old album's face,
Flip through the pages where time left its trace.
Photos of us, with smiles so wide,
Will rekindle the warmth I felt inside.
Or maybe I'll play a song we once knew,
One that reminds me of moments so true.
Each note a thread of a cherished threadbare,
Binding me to the days when you were there.
But I know this truth, though it breaks my heart,
Life's grand rhythm always pulls us apart.
You'll find new friends, new skies to explore,
And I'll stand at the shore, watching you soar.
Yet, how can I cling to a past that must fade,
When life's a dance where bonds are remade?
I'll carry your essence like a sunlit gleam,
Etched in the folds of my every dream.
The days of childhood, untainted by strife,
Were the most beautiful chapters of life.

Running through fields with no thought of the end,
Sharing our laughter with each loyal friend.
The warmth of the sun, the whispers of trees,
The songs of the birds carried on the breeze.
The games we played till the light turned low,
Moments so simple, yet they'd forever glow.
But life, my friend, is a river that flows,
It never stops, no matter who goes.
And though the tides may pull us away,
The essence of you in my heart will stay.
I'll meet new faces, craft bonds anew,
But none will compare to the days I had with you.
For the magic of childhood is a fleeting flame,
No other friendship will burn quite the same.
And yet, I embrace what the future will bring,
The cycle of life, its eternal spring.
New friends will come, as old ones depart,
But your place will remain, carved in my heart.
The sky turns orange as the sun takes its bow,
I sit by the window, reflecting on how
The seasons of life change with the breeze,
Like leaves that fall from the tallest trees.
This is the way of life's eternal lore,
To part and meet, and part once more.
For only when old bonds loosen their thread,
Can new ones be tied, where life's journey is led.
So go, my friend, let your wings take flight,
Chase your dreams through the starry night.
But remember the days when we ran through the stream,

For those are the days that we'll always dream.
Though time may scatter us far and wide,
You'll always be part of my heart's tide.
And when I look back on the years gone by,
I'll smile through tears, though I might still sigh.
Life is a story, with chapters anew,
And each one is precious, including you.
So farewell, my friend, though we drift apart,
You'll always reside in the depths of my heart.

103. The Storm's Warning

Before every storm, silence takes its throne,
A deep, dark quiet, where fears are sown.
We mistake its stillness for joy's embrace,
Not knowing the tempest is gathering pace.
The air hangs heavy, the skies turn gray,
Yet we dream of sunshine lighting the way.
Our hearts believe in a dawn so bright,
But shadows creep in, devouring the light.
How often are we deceived by hope,
Climbing dreams on a slippery slope.
We think tomorrow will heal the pain,
Yet find ourselves in the storm's domain.
The winds howl fierce, the thunder roars,
Breaking through life's fragile doors.
Chaos reigns where peace once lay,
And all our dreams are swept away.
No chance to run, no time to prepare,
The storm's fury is beyond compare.
It tears apart what we've built with care,
Leaving us shattered, gasping for air.
We crumble, we break, under its might,
Doubting the return of day from night.
The weight of despair feels endless, vast,
As if each breath may be our last.

But deep within, a whisper remains,
A voice that rises above the pain.
It says, "This is not your story's end,
The storm is here, but so is your strength, my friend."
The heart, though bruised, begins to beat,
A rhythm defiant, refusing defeat.
It whispers, "Rise, this is but the start,
More storms will come, but so will your heart."
For storms may ravage, but they cannot kill
The fire within, the unyielding will.
Each tempest leaves scars, but they're not in vain,
They teach us to endure, to dance in the rain.
The skies may fall, the earth may quake,
But the human spirit refuses to break.
From ashes we rise, like a phoenix born,
Facing each storm, though battered and worn.
Imagine the ocean after the tide,
The calm that comes when the storm subsides.
It whispers to you, in its gentle way,
"Survive the night, and you'll see the day."
The trees that bend but never snap,
The rivers that carve their own map.
Nature teaches us, time and again,
There's strength in endurance, and beauty in pain.
So let the storm rage, let it tear apart,
It cannot destroy the core of your heart.
For every tempest eventually fades,
Revealing the strength that courage made.

Stand tall, though the winds may scream,
Hold tight to hope, to life's fragile dream.
For after each storm, the skies will clear,
And a brighter dawn will draw near.
This is life's way, its eternal truth,
To test our spirit, to challenge our youth.
But through the trials, we learn to soar,
Braving the storms, stronger than before.
So when the silence warns of a storm ahead,
Don't cower in fear, don't be misled.
Prepare your soul, and embrace the fight,
For even the darkest storm gives way to light.

104. The Enigma of Beauty

O maiden of cascading hair, divine and free,

Whose footsteps echo like whispers through the sea.

Eyes so deep, they craft a spellbinding trance,

A mystery unfolds with each fleeting glance.

What mark do those enchanting eyes seek?

Whose soul trembles at the dreams they speak?

In every gathering, you grace the air,

Yet vanish like moonlight, beyond compare.

Your beauty spills like starlight's glow,

Wherever you wander, hearts overflow.

What magic do you weave, unseen, untold,

To captivate souls, young and old?

Perhaps the heavens sculpted you with care,

In moments stolen from eternity's glare.

For every heart seems to bow, undone,

By the radiance born of your sun.

You walk with grace, a dance untamed,

Like a peacock's stride, majestic, famed.

Your hair flows wild, like serpents in play,

A mesmerizing river at the break of day.

Each step you take, the world aligns,

A rhythmic pulse, the universe designs.

The path beneath you blooms with delight,

Dust turns to petals in your gentle might.

Your presence paints the skies in hues,
As if the heavens yearned to muse.
The winds pause to whisper your name,
The earth quivers, forever aflame.
A curious thought stirs every mind,
How can beauty be so unconfined?
A gift so rare, it feels divine,
As if sculpted by fate's perfect design.
Yet beauty like yours is more than skin,
It's a melody sung from deep within.
Each smile, a sunrise breaking the night,
Each glance, a promise of endless light.
But tell me, O muse, with charm untold,
What secrets lie in your heart's stronghold?
Do you wander seeking, or are you the sought,
A dream so vivid, yet never caught?
Perhaps your charm is a fleeting flame,
A dance of wonder, untamed, unclaimed.
Yet even flames leave warmth behind,
An eternal glow in every mind.
For beauty, they say, is a transient grace,
A fleeting shadow, time cannot trace.
But yours is a fire that refuses to wane,
An immortal spark that will always remain.
So walk, O enchantress, through life's grand hall,
Grace each moment, however small.
For every flower that blooms in your wake,
Knows beauty like yours is life's finest ache.

The world may wonder, the heavens may sigh,
At the mystery carried in your eye.
For beauty so pure cannot be confined,
It lives in the heart, eternal, divine.
And as you tread, a celestial muse,
Each step writes poetry, the world to enthuse.
A tale of wonder, a hymn so rare,
The enigma of beauty, beyond compare.

105. Whispers of the Moonlit Night

Tonight, I ask for your love, no denials, please,

Let us sit close, share words like the whispering breeze.

This night is radiant, dressed like a bride,

Her silvery veil glows, with stars as her pride.

Come near, let the silence between us dissolve,

In this perfect night, let our hearts evolve.

The jasmine-laden air carries secrets untold,

As we weave new dreams, both tender and bold.

The lake reflects the moon's serene face,

A mirror of stillness, of beauty and grace.

Ripples break softly, a gentle ballet,

As the night hums softly, holding time at bay.

Do you recall, how my gaze first found you?

Even then, I knew, this love would be true.

I saw the heavens within your eyes,

A treasure no earthly wealth could ever buy.

The breeze wraps around us like a lover's embrace,

The stars above watch, blessings in their place.

Every glance at you is a prayer divine,

Every heartbeat of mine longs to intertwine.

This night feels eternal, as though time has paused,

An immortal moment where love is embossed.

Sit with me by the lake, where shadows sleep,
Let us talk until dawn begins to seep.
The trees sway gently, their whispers align,
With the rhythm of hearts, with love's design.
Even the crickets soften their song,
As if knowing we've waited for this all along.
The moon casts her glow on your face so dear,
A light so soft, it erases all fear.
I've loved you before, in lives I can't trace,
And I'll love you again, in every time and space.
This night is ours, no one else can intrude,
A sanctified silence, an enchanting mood.
No voices, no noise, just our breaths in sync,
As the stars above begin to blink.
Your beauty eternal, untouched by years,
A muse to my hopes, a cure to my fears.
Your presence alone makes the world fade,
In this celestial night, love's foundation is laid.
Let's sit on the rocks by the lake's quiet shore,
Exchange our dreams, and wish for more.
The water whispers tales of ancient times,
Echoing softly in rhythmic chimes.
Let us linger here, in this night's embrace,
Two souls entwined in a sacred space.
The world may fade, and moments may flee,
But this night will stay, etched in eternity.
So I ask again, love, grant me your heart,
In this perfect night, let us never part.
Let this moment endure, let it stay divine,

For tonight, and forever, you'll always be mine.

106. The Journey's Song

Upon this road where echoes sing,
Through golden fields where breezes cling,
A journey vast, yet light as air,
Where moments dance without a care.
The trees stand tall with arms so wide,
Their emerald whispers side by side,
Casting shadows, cool and deep,
Where weary hearts may rest and keep.
A silver brook in laughter flows,
Mirroring skies in soft repose,
Pebbles glisten where waters play,
As if the stars had fallen astray.
The fragrance of earth, fresh and new,
Wrapped in morning's misty dew,
Calls the wanderer to behold,
A tale of wonders, bright and bold.
Through rustling leaves, the whispers rise,
A symphony of nature's ties,
The song of winds, the hum of trees,
A lullaby of tranquil seas.
Lo! A deer in fleeting grace,
Leaps through the meadow's warm embrace,
A spirit wild, yet free and bright,
Boundless as the golden light.

O why should I, with restless feet,
March on past wonders rich and sweet?
Each blade of grass, each rolling hill,
Invites the soul to pause and fill.
For time is still where beauty stays,
In golden light of drifting days,
A dream embraced, a thought unchained,
A life beyond what fate ordained.
"Rest, O traveller, pause and see,
This moment's breath, eternity.
Why chase the dawn? Why chase the dusk?
Let life be held, let life be trust."
A voice so soft, yet firm and wise,
Rises through the deep blue skies,
Telling tales of paths untold,
Not just of silver, not just of gold.
For what is journey, if not a song?
A place to stay, to feel, belong?
Not just the end, but steps so bright,
Each whispering breeze, each ray of light.
Should I run, should I race?
Or let the wind caress my face?
Should I seek what lies ahead?
Or cherish where my feet have tread?
The sun spills gold on earth so vast,
Yet only moments truly last,
A fleeting joy, a passing pain,
Yet each returns in time again.

The flowers bloom, the birds take flight,
The heavens paint their hues so bright,
Yet eyes that chase tomorrow's gleam,
May lose today, lost in a dream.
So here I stand, with heart set free,
A wanderer of destiny,
Not bound by time, nor held by space,
But lost within this world's embrace.
O journey bright, O pathway wise,
With endless love in boundless skies,
Take me not beyond too soon,
Let me stay and dance with noon.
For life's not made of far and near,
But moments held, so bright, so clear,
A whispered song, a fleeting call,
A time to love, a time for all.
So let me pause, let me be,
Where time dissolves and I am free,
For every step, for every sight,
Is but a piece of endless light.

107. The Eternal Flow of Time

The present hums, the past is gone,
The future waits, yet stays unknown.
A fleeting breath, a drifting stream,
A wisp of life, a wandering dream.
What's mine today may not remain,
The tides may turn, the path may wane.
No hands can grasp the sands of fate,
Yet hearts still yearn, and hope elates.
The sky unfurls in golden hue,
Soft clouds drift where whispers grew.
The trees stand firm yet sway so free,
Echoing life's philosophy.
A stream meanders, clear and bright,
Reflecting moments bathed in light.
But waters rush, they do not stay,
They dance, they leap, then fade away.
Companions walk, then part their way,
For none may hold the dawn or day.
Still, voices linger in the air,
A trace of love, a silent prayer.
Alone we came, alone we leave,
Yet bind our hearts, our oaths believe.

Through fleeting time, we make our stand,
Though dust will claim our feet and hands.
Not gold, nor toil can change the tide,
Yet choices shape the way we ride.
The wind may howl, the storm may break,
Yet strength is found in hearts awake.
The setting sun, the moon's embrace,
Remind us all of time's soft grace.
The world will turn, the past will fade,
Yet love remains—a light unstayed.
So take this breath, embrace this time,
No hour returns, no bells rewind.
Let moments bloom, let voices sing,
For life's a bird on fleeting wing.

108. Whispers of the Moonlit Night

What is it about tonight's moonlight,
That turns the darkness into something bright?
A silver glow spills across the sky,
Filling the soul with a peaceful sigh.
I had stepped out, craving the unknown,
To walk for miles, to be alone.
To feel the breeze, cool and light,
To wander beneath this velvet night.
But now beneath this tender gleam,
I find no urge to chase a dream.
The road ahead can wait till dawn,
Tonight, I'll let my soul be drawn.
By the silent lake, I take my place,
Where ripples dance in moon's embrace.
The waters hum a lullaby low,
Reflecting stars in endless flow.
Above, the moon drifts slow and wise,
A silver beacon in the skies.
I watch it gleam, I watch it sway,
As smoke curls up and fades away.
A cigarette burns between my lips,
A slow inhale, a soft eclipse.

I trace the air with rings so thin,
Like fleeting dreams they swirl within.
The radio hums a lover's tune,
A serenade beneath the moon.
Soft melodies that stir the night,
Filling the air with love's delight.
I hum along, I close my eyes,
And drift away where silence lies.
A world where time moves soft and slow,
Where only hearts and echoes glow.
The city sleeps, the stars stand tall,
The night wraps me in its thrall.
A distant thought, a lost embrace,
Lingers softly in this space.
No voices call, no steps intrude,
Just me, the night, and solitude.
The wind caresses, cool and light,
A lover's touch, a sweet respite.
And so I sit, just breathing deep,
Watching the sky, hearing it weep.
The moon a poet, whispering low,
Stories only dreamers know.
Through cigarette smoke and fading songs,
I wonder where my soul belongs.
In endless night or breaking dawn,
Or in the echoes long since gone?
Yet here I stay, unchained, untied,
With stars above and time beside.
In love with life, in love with now,

Beneath the moon's eternal vow.

109. A Life Less Ordinary

They dance in golden halls of mirth,
In laughter's glow, by fires bright,
A home adorned in warmth and hearth,
With joy that echoes through the night.
Their days are soft, their paths are clear,
No storm to shake, no winds to veer.
A life of comfort, safe and sweet,
Where every dream finds rest complete.
Yet in my chest, a fire burns,
A restless call, a soul that yearns.
Not for silk or golden wine,
But cliffs to climb, and stars to shine.
I crave the wild, the endless sky,
The roaring waves where sea birds fly.
A life untamed, fierce and free,
Where every step is destiny.
I dream of peaks where ice winds sing,
Of glaciers carved by winter's wing.
To stand atop a world so white,
And touch the clouds, defying height.
To feel the earth beneath my hand,
The frozen breath, the boundless land.
No walls, no chains, no rigid ties,
Only the wind and endless skies.

I long to sail the raging tide,

Upon a raft with stars as guide.

Through storms that crash with wrath untold,

Through lightning's dance, through waters cold.

To see the dawn from ocean's crest,

To test my will in fate's own test.

Not safe, not still, but wild and bright,

A heart ablaze in nature's might.

To dwell within the jungle deep,

Where ancient spirits watch and keep.

To build a home on boughs so high,

Where vines embrace the endless sky.

To hear the whisper of the trees,

The murmured tales upon the breeze.

Where moonlight weaves through emerald shade,

A world untouched, a dream unmade.

Yet here I stand, feet tied in stone,

A heart that longs, yet stands alone.

For what I seek demands a price,

A leap of faith, a roll of dice.

To leave behind the warmth, the known,

The steady ground I call my own.

For out beyond the simple way,

Lies night and storm and pathless gray.

Am I a fool to dream so bold,

To trade the hearth for winds so cold?

To walk away from certain peace,

For fleeting moments none may seize?

I do not wear the hero's name,

I fear the fall, the risk, the flame.
Yet in my veins, the tempest sways,
A whisper calls, a song of days.
A life less ordinary waits,
Beyond the doors, beyond the gates.
Not in crowns, nor in the throne,
But in the dust, in paths unknown.
To live not safe, but to be free,
To carve my tale in memory.
For though the fear may hold me tight,
My soul still longs to touch the height.
So let me rise, let fear be still,
For dreams will burn, but not be killed.
A gladiator, blade in hand,
Fighting fate with courage grand.
A wanderer upon the seas,
A seeker lost in ancient trees.
Not just to live, but to be wild,
A tempest's heart, a dreamer's child.
For life is not in gold or gain,
But in the thunder, in the rain.
In roaring waves, in mountains tall,
In risking all—to have it all.

110. Whispers of Time

Time drifts like a silent river, slow and unchained,
Carving valleys deep where memories remained.
Once familiar hands slip into the mist,
Strangers walk beside me, fate's quiet twist.
The dawn that once held promises untold,
Has passed like echoes in chambers cold.
The wheel of time turns, relentless, blind,
Some things we seek, yet never find.
I reach for moments, only to see them fade,
Like golden autumn leaves in twilight's cascade.
The more I grasp, the more they flee,
Like whispers lost in a restless sea.
The past lingers in the hush of the rain,
Drumming against my windowpane.
A storm-tossed night, wild and free,
Carrying voices that once spoke to me.
I wander alone where memories grow,
A house once mine, now dust and shadow.
Walls that heard my laughter bright,
Stand in silence, robbed of light.
How far I've come, how far I go,
From childhood's fields to winter's snow.
Once I danced where the lilies swayed,
Now I lean on a staff, weathered, decayed.

Once, my cries could summon her near,
My mother, my home, my cradle dear.
Now, though my voice shatters the air,
She does not come, she is not there.
The wind hums songs of yesteryears,
A lullaby laced with unshed tears.
Moonlight spills on cobbled lanes,
Tracing the steps of joy and pain.
The old oak creaks, whispering tales,
Of dreams that rode on fleeting sails.
The scent of jasmine, soft and deep,
Stirs the embers of love I keep.
The night is heavy, yet stars still shine,
Holding the past in a thread divine.
In their glow, I hear the call,
To rise once more, to stand tall.
For time may steal, but it also sows,
In empty fields, new life still grows.
The road ahead, though wrapped in mist,
Holds a promise fate has kissed.
So I walk on, with steady grace,
Through seasons swift in time's embrace.
What once was lost, may yet remain,
For time returns all—again and again.

111. Endless Journey of Love

Hand in hand, we walk ahead,
No maps to guide, no words unsaid.
Life flows like a wandering stream,
No grand purpose, no golden dream.
Yet with you beside, my steps feel light,
In endless dusk, in silver light.
No path is carved, no fate is drawn,
Yet life hums on from dusk to dawn.
The world may say we chase the dust,
That love alone is not enough.
But let them mock, let them stare,
For in your eyes, I find my air.
Through city streets, through fields so wide,
Through mountains tall, by ocean's tide.
We roam like birds with broken chains,
Dancing wild in summer rains.
Each droplet sings, each puddle gleams,
Our laughter spills like lucid streams.
Beneath the clouds so dark and deep,
We let the storm our secrets keep.
Winds may howl and thunder call,
Yet wrapped in love, we fear no fall.
For hearts that beat in perfect tune,
Turn every storm into a monsoon.

Barefoot upon the thirsty sands,
We run where none have left their hands.
A desert vast, a sunlit trance,
Yet love gives thirst a second chance.
No home to claim, no walls to bind,
Yet in your arms, my peace I find.
A lonely deer, lost and worn,
Finds a stream, no more forlorn.
So too are we, in fate's embrace,
Finding love in time's vast space.
Not bound by laws, nor weighed by past,
Just moving free, just breathing fast.
People wonder, people sigh,
How do we smile, with nothing nigh?
No palace tall, no silver chain,
Yet richer still in love's refrain.
For wealth is found in fleeting sights,
In morning mist, in velvet nights.
Come, my love, the road extends,
Beyond the dusk where starlight bends.
No need to pause, no need to rest,
For in your love, I am my best.
Through rain or sun, through dust or snow,
With you beside, my heart will glow.
Let the world chase fleeting gold,
Let them barter love for tales untold.
We shall wander, hearts entwined,
Two free spirits, undefined.
No final stop, no end to see,

Just you and me, eternally free.

112. Whispers of a Timeless Love

Do not leave me restless so soon,

Swear upon love, return by the moon.

See how the flowers blush and sigh,

As your beauty graces the sky.

Soft petals tremble in morning light,

Afraid to wither in your sight.

Walk slowly, my love, stay a while,

Let me drink the warmth of your smile.

The breeze entwines your raven hair,

Weaving whispers, light as air.

Oh, let not the evening steal you away,

For dawn has just begun to play.

Look, the butterflies sip with grace,

Honeyed nectar in love's embrace.

The koel sings a tune so sweet,

A melody spun at your feet.

Even the clouds halt in the sky,

Shielding you from the sun's bold eye.

Time stands still as you walk past,

Each step an echo meant to last.

Oh, pause a moment, let me see,

Your beauty wrapped in poetry.

Let me gaze before you go,
And drink your presence, soft and slow.
Oh, love, the world is but a stage,
Where we play within time's cage.
Yet in your eyes, I see a land,
Where love is endless, hand in hand.
So stay, my love, just for a while,
Let me drown in your sweet smile.
Let the rivers run, the forests wake,
Let love be all that hearts partake.
The sky may turn from gold to gray,
But love like ours shall never stray.
Even if the winds may call,
Hold my hand, embrace it all.
Barefoot, we trace the silver sand,
Dreamers lost in a foreign land.
No roof, no walls, no home to name,
Yet love alone keeps us the same.
The world may question, scorn, and stare,
Yet love is freedom, pure and rare.
Stay, my love, let echoes ring,
Let our love be an endless spring.
Drink the rain, embrace the night,
Hold me close till morning light.
For love is not just fleeting years,
But whispered songs and fallen tears.
The earth shall fade, the stars may fall,
But love will echo through it all.
As long as skies remain so blue,

DO WE LIVE, OR JUST EXIST?

I shall forever wait for you.

113. The Journey of Life

Upon this road of dust and dreams,
Where silent echoes call our names,
We walk as strangers lost in time,
No map, no path, no guiding flame.
Some tread with love beside their own,
Hand in hand, step by step,
While others drift like fallen leaves,
Alone, unfelt, and unwept.
A lotus bud that never bloomed,
Swallowed by a cruel breeze,
Like souls who never truly lived,
Stolen by fate's unseen disease.
Some draw breath yet never taste
The sweetness life was meant to bring,
Trapped in chains of hollow days,
Echoes lost, unheard, unseen.
They have the gold, the finest silk,
The world bows low beneath their feet,
Yet in their hands, they beg for time,
A moment more, a breath to keep.
We come alone, we stay a while,
We weave our dreams in borrowed light,
But when the call of dusk arrives,
We fade into the endless night.

Once, the voices cried my name,
Now silence hums where echoes lay,
The poet's words dissolve in air,
Like mist that dawn has chased away.
Like fleeting winds upon the shore,
Like ripples swallowed by the sea,
A whisper lost, a breath expired,
A song unclaimed by memory.
O wanderer, lost upon this way,
Do not seek to understand,
For life is but a broken stream,
That slips like dust between our hands.
Yet live, and love, and dance, and dream,
Before the winds call out your name,
For in the end, when all is gone,
No road returns, no voice remains.
So walk, my friend, but leave no chains,
No bitter cries, no weight of pain,
For life was never ours to own,
But only ours to touch… and wane.

114. Through Storms, We Laugh and Live

The clouds rolled in, dark and dense,

A rumbling sky, a storm immense.

The wind howled through the narrow street,

As rain came crashing, wild and sweet.

No umbrellas, no hasty run,

Just you and I, and a world undone.

Barefoot splashes, puddles deep,

The town's awake, but half asleep.

Rickshaw bells, a dog's loud bark,

Streetlights flicker in the misty dark.

A chaiwala hums his old refrain,

Pouring warmth through sheets of rain.

We stand like fools, drenched and free,

Laughing hard at destiny.

If fate throws storms with all its might,

We'll dance beneath the thundering night!

No shadow lingers, no friend in sight,

Yet hand in hand, we hold on tight.

If troubles rise like tides so high,

We'll ride the waves, we won't deny.

For life's a ride on a leaky boat,

Sometimes it sinks, sometimes it floats.

But who needs sails when love is strong?
We'll hum a tune and drift along!
The rain beats down on rooftops old,
Market stalls in colours bold.
People rush, but we just stay,
Two mad dreamers lost in play.
A gust of wind, a power cut—
Street's gone dark, but we care not.
By lantern's glow, a poet writes,
Of hearts that dance on stormy nights.
The tea is hot, the groundnuts crisp,
Crunching loud through thunder's hiss.
A simple meal, yet rich in taste,
For joy is found in love, not haste.
A downpour fierce, a sky so wild,
Yet we stand strong, like fate's own child.
Through winds that roar and tempests swell,
We'll find a way, we'll weather well.
For even if we're torn apart,
Like scattered leaves in a storm's restart,
We'll find our way, we'll meet again,
Like rivers rushing back to rain.
So let the storm cry out in vain,
Let lightning strike and shake the plain.
We have no fear, we have no doubt,
For love's a flame that won't burn out.
And if the night turns cold and bleak,
If shadows loom and spirits weep,
We'll find a tree, we'll sit beneath,

And share a dream, a laugh, a peace.
For what is life but fleeting rain?
A storm, a sip, a love, a pain.
So hold my hand, let's face the tide,
With silly grins and hearts held wide!

115. Whispers of a Fool's Heart

The world spins slow, as I stand lost in your thought,
A thousand stars lighting the night, yet my mind is caught,
Your smile—oh, how it makes the dark sky blush,
A gentle wave of moonlight turns into a sacred hush.
In the silence of a storm that brews beneath the moon,
I find my heart shattered, yet content to swoon,
Like the finest wine, bittersweet and divine,
I drink the remnants of your love, lost in time.
In the moments we never shared, I weep yet I smile,
The beauty of your love is a journey, a thousand miles,
Unseen, untasted, but a longing so real,
An emotion I cannot deny, a wound I must heal.
Beneath the veil of night, in the warmth of your absence,
I stand, a fool in love with dreams and pretense,
Your love, a distant echo, yet I cannot refrain,
A wounded soul, walking through love's endless pain.
You, the muse of my every verse, a phantom I chase,
A lover whose shadow, I can never embrace,
Yet here I stand, a man who never forgets,
Chasing your whispers like the setting sun's regret.
A kiss you never gave, a glance you never threw,
Yet I wait, as if the world began with you.

You may never be mine, and I know that truth,
But still, I stand here, wearing love's broken youth.
Oh, the world mocks me, in every cold sigh,
Tells me I'm lost, tells me to say goodbye,
But with every tear, I rise again,
A fool for your love, a man without pain.
For in the quiet of the night, I speak to the stars,
I wish for your love, no matter how far,
In every universe, in every space,
I'll wait for you with love, though time we cannot trace.
I may never hold you, I may never see,
But in my heart, you are all that's free.
No one will understand, and they call me insane,
But in this madness, I find my reign.
The wine, though bitter, is sweeter still,
As I remember the dream, the unspoken thrill.
For what is love if not a silent prayer,
A longing, a cry, a hope that hangs in the air?
So I stand, a man with a heart broken wide,
Sipping the red wine of love, with nothing to hide.
For though the world calls me foolish and blind,
I'd rather be lost in love than leave it behind.
And as I wander in the depth of my soul's song,
I'll wait for your glance, where it belongs,
For in the endless sky, my heart will soar,
And I will love you forevermore.
In your name, I find my peace and pain,
In your absence, I'm broken yet remain.
Oh, love, cruel and kind, your gift is true,

And though you never come, I will wait for you.
So here I stand, foolish, but alive,
Sipping on dreams that help me survive.
For though you may never turn to me,
In my heart, you are all that I see.
The world may say I'm lost, and I may be blind,
But my heart knows the path, and I don't mind.
I'll wait for you in the shadows of night,
For you are the sun, and I am your light.

116. Whisper of the Last Night

Oh fleeting time, slow your pace,
Hold these moments in your embrace.
The dawn is cruel, it waits for none,
But let me steal a breath before it's gone.
The lantern sways in the quiet air,
Its trembling glow—our love laid bare.
The night hums low, the crickets sing,
Yet silence wraps us in its wing.
Her eyes, two stars in the midnight deep,
Hold storms within, yet dare not weep.
She traces lines upon my skin,
As if to etch them deep within.
Her voice—so soft, so barely heard,
A whisper lost within a word.
"Must you go?" she breathes, so light,
As if her plea could halt the night.
I brush my fingers through her hair,
Like wind that drifts through fields laid bare.
"I must," I say, though words betray,
For heart and duty pull away.
The world beyond this fragile room,
Lies painted red with war and doom.

The border calls, the bugles cry,
Beneath the vast, indifferent sky.
But here—within these walls of love,
Beneath the stars that shine above,
We hold the night as if it's gold,
A tale of love, too deep, untold.
Her hands, like autumn's fading leaves,
Clutch mine, refusing to release.
"If you must go, then take my soul,
For life without you is not whole."
The wind sighs soft against the door,
As if it too would plead for more.
The bed, the sheets, the moonlight dim,
All whisper stories lost in hymn.
I press my lips upon her brow,
A soldier's promise, sacred vow.
"Though distance spreads its cruel divide,
My heart shall march close by your side."
She nods, though silent tears still fall,
Like raindrops weeping through the hall.
The walls remember, the floorboards creak,
As if they too have hearts that speak.
The candle flickers, bends, and sways,
Its light dissolving into haze.
The night, though long, is slipping fast,
A love too pure, too vast to last.
"If fate is kind," I tell her low,
"I'll find my way through fire and snow.
And if I don't, then do not cry,

For love like ours will never die."
She pulls me close, her breath, her skin,
A warmth that wars cannot rescind.
For in this moment, wide and deep,
Two souls entwine where echoes weep.
The morning waits, the sky turns pale,
The call of war, the distant wail.
Yet still I linger, hush and tight,
A thief who steals one last goodnight.
So time, I beg—just one more hour,
Before fate claims what's not yet ours.
Let love defy the winds of war,
And be our shield forevermore.

117. Whispers of Light and Ash

In halls of gold where echoes dance,
Beneath the vault of fate's expanse,
A thousand voices rise and fall,
Their fleeting cries—one, then all.
A sea of hands, of pleading souls,
Grasping toward celestial goals,
Yet light departs, and love decays,
As time dissolves in misty haze.
Once we stood as stars entwined,
Our laughter etched in fate's design,
Through endless dawns, through sleepless night,
Bound by fire, fierce and bright.
Oh, love that shone in tempest's wake,
That none could tarnish, none could break,
Now slips like sand through fingers tight,
A ghost of warmth, a stolen light.
And friendship, bold with banners high,
Once soared with wings against the sky,
Now fragments torn in battle's breath,
Now shattered glass upon the depths.
We built our dreams with trembling hands,
Upon the bones of shifting sands,

But winds have howled, and tempests raged,
And love is lost, and war is waged.
O friend, O heart, I hear you still,
A voice that haunts, a whisper shrill,
Among the clouds, beyond the veil,
A shadow cast, a mournful tale.
Above, the heavens split apart,
With golden wings and bleeding stars,
They rise, they soar, they break the chains,
As mortals grasp at love's remains.
Some reach for light, some drown in woe,
Some find the path, yet none can know,
If what they loved, what once was whole,
Still lingers bright, or fades in soul.
For love is war, and loss is gain,
And joy is laced with threads of pain,
We give, we hold, we yearn, we trust,
Then turn to embers, fall to dust.
Yet in that fall, in sorrow deep,
When all seems lost, when none may keep,
A whisper calls through night's embrace,
A touch unseen, a fleeting trace.
The ones we love, though torn, apart,
Still carve their names upon the heart,
Not lost, not gone, but changed anew,
In stardust skies, in morning dew.
So mourn not love, nor friendship's wane,
Nor loss that bends the soul in pain,
For light returns where dark has been,

And love, once given, burns within.

118. The Scarlet Dream

One day, I pondered, what is beauty's face?
Is it the hush of dawn, the moon's embrace?
Or does it dwell in fleeting things—
A whispered name, the hush of wings?
I saw her then, a vision bright,
Bathed in dusk's half-mourning light.
She walked through fields where silence grew,
Where time stood still in drops of dew.
A scarlet dress, the hue of fire,
Draped like a dream, like lost desire.
It kissed the earth with every tread,
A river flowing, fierce and red.
Her golden hair, a waterfall,
Cascading, endless, wild, and tall.
Braided light that brushed her knees,
A sunbeam caught in wayward breeze.
Her ears, like whispers finely spun,
Carved by fate, by elven tongue.
Each curve a song, a siren's call,
A melody that stilled them all.
Her skin was moonlight, soft and fair,
A tale unwritten in the air.
And on her lips, a breathless hue,
The dusk and dawn in crimson fused.

Her eyes—oh, eyes of piercing blue!
Twin sapphires dipped in morning's dew.
They saw the stars before they shone,
They knew the songs the winds had known.
She walked in silence, yet the ground,
Bent low beneath her, lost and bound.
The autumn leaves in rustling prayer,
Reached forth and wove into her hair.
Her fingers traced the world unseen,
A poet's thought, a longing keen.
With every step, the flowers swayed,
Enchanted by the spell she laid.
Oh, love! If love had ever been,
It lived within this silent queen.
Not in the vows of fleeting breath,
But in the way she conquered death.
For beauty was not meant to stay,
It fades like embers swept away.
Yet in her wake, the heavens sighed,
As though the gods themselves had cried.
She turned to me, her gaze like fire,
And I, a fool, a lost admirer.
For love is brief, and fate unkind,
And beauty stays not with the blind.
I reached for her, my hands in vain,
Yet grasped but echoes, dust, and rain.
For what is love, if not a dream?
A phantom seen in scarlet gleam.

And yet I knew, though time would fade,
Though winter stole what autumn made,
That somewhere, 'neath the endless skies,
Her scarlet dress still billows wide.
And in my heart, where dreams take flight,
She walks through fields of endless light.
Not bound by time, nor lost in fate,
But waiting at love's final gate.
So tell me now, if beauty's true,
If love remains in skies of blue—
Is she but wind? A fleeting sigh?
Or does she live beyond goodbye?

119. Whispers to the Stars

The night is deep, the world is still,
Moonless sky, a hollow chill.
They slumber soft in love's embrace,
But wakefulness has found my place.
Stars above in velvet spread,
Glisten softly, words unsaid.
I weave my thoughts in silver threads,
To tie them where the silence treads.
Each star a whisper, faint and true,
Of hearts that break, of skies so blue.
Of love that lingers, love that fades,
Of journeys lost in twilight shades.
The wind hums low, it sings, it sighs,
A lullaby for closed-up eyes.
But sleep has fled my weary chest,
As longing carves a hollow nest.
For somewhere far, a voice remains,
A name I murmur, soft with pain.
Does it echo past the seas?
Or vanish like a broken breeze?
The lamp within my soul grows weak,
A trembling flame too dim to speak.
I press my palm against my chest,
To cage the storm, to still unrest.

The night has hands, it holds me tight,
An unseen whisper in the night.
Yet all the world, so careless free,
Drifts away in dreams but me.
I count the stars, I count in vain,
For they are many, none the same.
Some are distant, cold, and bright,
Some are ghosts of vanished light.
Much like love, much like time,
Leaving echoes, lost in rhyme.
I sit beneath this endless sky,
A fleeting thought, a wondering sigh.
The walls are silent, closed and bare,
The window sings a song of air.
The moon has gone, the night is blind,
But still it reads my aching mind.
Will dawn arrive with golden hands,
And touch my soul with light's commands?
Or will I stay, as shadows do,
Between the dark and morning's hue?
I close my eyes, I make no sound,
The night is vast, yet I am bound.
Perhaps I too, am just a spark,
A fading glow in endless dark.

120. A Dream That Walks Away

She must wait somewhere, unknown, unseen,

A fleeting ghost in a world between.

I search for her in every street,

In nameless crowds, in echoes sweet.

Perhaps she hums a song at night,

A tune that fades with morning's light.

Perhaps she steps into my dreams,

A whispered name, a voice that gleams.

She walks through mist, she drifts like air,

I call, but silence lingers there.

I beg her—stay, let night remain,

Let stars not fade, let time refrain.

Yet like a sigh, like breath set free,

She slips beyond, away from me.

A wisp of dawn, a shadow lost,

A wish denied at fate's own cost.

How many nights must pass me by,

Before she stays, before she sighs?

Before she leans, before she speaks,

Before I touch the dream I seek?

Does she know the words I say,

When sleep dissolves and night turns gray?

Does she hear the songs I weave,
Or feel the longing as I grieve?
I wonder if the day will come,
When fate relents, when hearts succumb.
When time no longer turns away,
And she will sit with me and stay.
Will truth and dreams then intertwine?
Will she be hers, will I be mine?
Or will my breath, lost and weak,
Be drowned in beauty I dare not speak?
For if she comes, if she is near,
I'll lose myself, dissolve in fear.
No longer man, nor flesh, nor soul,
Just longing's fire without control.
I would not blink, I would not move,
I'd be a verse, a whispered proof.
Of love that never touched the day,
Yet in the dark still finds its way.
And if she asks me, must I go?
I'll tell her no, stay, let time slow.
Let night stretch long, let moments bend,
For dreams like her must never end.
But if she fades, if she must leave,
Then let me go, let me believe—
That somewhere lost in time's embrace,
She waits for me in some far place.
And I will walk, I will roam,
Through every street, through every home.
Through every wind, through endless skies,

DO WE LIVE, OR JUST EXIST?

Chasing dreams that never die.

121. The Donkey's Question

Beneath the glow of neon light,
Through streets alive with song and sight,
A donkey walks on weary feet,
Paraded down the crowded street.
His bray is lost in laughter's swell,
A photo's price—a tale to sell.
A garland rests upon his mane,
A crown of joy, a mark of pain.
His hooves once knew the quiet land,
The rolling hills, the golden sand.
He carried burdens, heavy loads,
Along the sunlit, dusty roads.
Yet now he walks where voices rise,
Where glass and steel eclipse the skies.
His purpose not to plow nor roam,
But stand for strangers far from home.
They smile, they laugh, they stroke his side,
A living prop for fleeting pride.
They pay, they pose, they turn away,
Forgetting him within the day.
But does he dream when night is near?
Of fields where silence soothes the ear?
Of open skies where dawn unfolds,
Where earth is soft and grass is gold?

Or does he feel the weight of men,
The hands, the chains, the world again?
Does he still know the taste of free?
Or is he lost to memory?
I watch him stand with solemn grace,
A soul misplaced, a nameless face.
My heart rebels, my mind resists—
Do I see more than he exists?
A moment's guilt, a whispered doubt,
Then music swells and drowns it out.
The dancers twirl, the glasses clink,
And thoughts grow faint with food and drink.
But still, the question lingers on—
Where does the line lie, crossed or drawn?
Do hands that feed still hold a chain?
Is pleasure built on silent pain?
The circus, stage, the gilded cage,
The lion bowed, the dolphin's stage.
The horses bound in hoops of fire,
The eagle tamed, its wings retired.
The line is blurred, the choice unclear,
Between our love and what we fear.
We claim to care, we say they're ours,
Yet trade their freedom for our hours.
The donkey walks as donkeys do,
Through dust, through light, through me and you.
No words he speaks, yet still he knows,
The weight of all the world he tows.

And when the music fades to rest,
And stars ignite the ocean's crest,
He dreams of something vast and free,
A world beyond captivity.
For all he's known is hoof and chain,
A life of work, a life of pain.
And yet he walks, and yet he brays,
And hopes for kinder, brighter days.
If he could ask, what would he say?
Would he forgive, or turn away?
Would he still trust, or would he see,
That freedom's price is memory?
I leave, my mind a troubled sea,
Still hearing hooves behind of me.
The donkey stands beneath the night,
A question formed in silent light.
And though the world may turn aside,
I walk away, but not inside.
For somewhere deep, I hear his call—
A voice that asks the price of all.

122. The Puzzle of Life

Life's a riddle, strange and deep,
A tale of sorrow, a dreamless sleep.
When I stand, with breath in me,
No soul to care, no eyes to see.
I call for aid, I reach in vain,
But hands withdraw, hearts refrain.
No time they spare, no pause they take,
No words of love, no bonds to make.
Yet when the winds of fate do call,
And death's cold shadow starts to fall,
They'll gather round in mournful grace,
With solemn tears upon their face.
Where were they when days were long?
When I had dreams, when I was strong?
Where were they when nights grew cold?
When I sought warmth, when I felt old?
I lay in sickness, weak and bare,
But no one came, no one cared.
No whispers soft, no gentle touch,
A life alone, a fate so much.
Yet when the fire claims my form,
They'll come in crowds, a grieving storm.
With heavy hearts, with voices low,
They'll speak of love they never showed.

"Oh, if we had just one more day,
To sit with you, to laugh, to stay…
Oh, if we had just known your pain,
We'd walk with you through sun and rain."
But time is cruel, and truth is clear,
The love they speak is not sincere.
For where was love when I was near?
Where was love when I was here?
They'll light the flames, they'll bow in shame,
But I will not hear, I'll have no name.
Their voices lost in smoky skies,
Their empty grief, their hollow cries.
So love me now, while breath remains,
Before I leave, before it wanes.
Sit with me beneath the moon,
For morning comes, and then too soon…
I'll be a whisper in the past,
A fleeting shadow fading fast.
And all the tears that fall too late,
Shall never change my silent fate.

123. The Curse of the Tides

In Torrak's bay where cold winds weep,
A village rests in slumber deep.
By day they toil, by night they dream,
Where lanterns cast a golden gleam.
The fishermen brave, with hands so worn,
Sailed the tides before the morn.
Their boats like shadows skimmed the waves,
Seeking fortune, daring graves.
The sea was kind, the sea was cruel,
It played no games, it followed no rule.
Some nights it whispered, soft and low,
Some nights it roared with wrathful woe.
And in the eve, by fire's embrace,
Old Felric spoke of times erased.
Of kings now dust, of treasures drowned,
Of secrets lost beneath the ground.
But on this night, with stormwinds high,
His voice was grave, his warnings nigh.
"Do not sail, for fate is grim,
The mermaids call with luring hymn."
The village laughed, they scoffed, they jeered,
"Mermaids? Old man, you've aged in fear!"
Yet as they left, his words remained,
A whisper deep, a fate ordained.

Through raging dark, the storm did grow,
Waves like beasts began to throw.
Yet in the wind, a song was spun,
A wailing tune, a haunting one.
The fishermen, with hearts ensnared,
Followed notes so sweet, so rare.
A melody both bright and bleak,
That kissed their minds and bid them seek.
Deeper still, they rode the tide,
Blinded fools by voices wide.
Eyes of silver, lips so red,
Hair like moonlight, bodies fed.
The mermaids danced with beckoning grace,
A timeless hunger on their face.
One by one, the men succumbed,
In water's arms, their fates were strummed.
The dawn arose with golden hue,
The storm was spent, the sky was blue.
On empty boats, the nets lay bare,
But where were those who once stood there?
No cries of joy, no laughter bright,
No voices rose to greet the light.
The village wept, the wives did wail,
For none returned to tell the tale.
And old man Felric, frail and wise,
Watched the sea with knowing eyes.
For those who mock the whispered lore,
Are claimed by tides forevermore.

124. Angels in Disguise

Once upon a time, in a town so bright,
Where lanterns danced with golden light,
Three little pigs, in coats so neat,
Walked down the bustling, cobbled street.
Hooves clattered and feathers swayed,
As peacocks twirled in grand parade.
Giraffes bent low to greet the day,
While goats and hens found games to play.
The market shimmered, filled with cheer,
For Christmas Eve had drawn so near.
Bakeries spilled their sugared scent,
Through air where songs of joy were sent.
"Meat and buns, and cakes so sweet,
For Grandma's feast, a Christmas treat!"
The youngest piglet laughed and twirled,
As colours burst throughout the world.
But by a shadowed alley's end,
A tiger sat, with bones that bent.
His fur was torn, his eyes were weak,
His voice came out—a hollow streak.
"Oh kind ones, spare a crumb or two,
I have no home, no feast, no stew.
Once I roared and ruled with pride,
Now hunger clings and won't subside."

The pigs stepped back, their hearts unsure,
For teeth still gleamed, though weak and poor.
They turned away, their task in mind,
But guilt was trailing close behind.
Yet as they walked past shining stores,
Where lights adorned the festive doors,
A whisper deep within them grew,
"A feast means nothing if love is few."
The youngest turned, his eyes now bright,
His brothers followed, hearts turned light.
Back they ran through crowded lanes,
Past carriages, past candy canes.
"Wait, old tiger, please don't stray,
Tonight no soul should fade away."
With every coin, they bought him bread,
Warm spiced rolls and soup so red.
Fruits so ripe and cakes so round,
A feast where kindness could be found.
The tiger ate with grateful eyes,
As stars reflected in the skies.
But as the last of coins were spent,
The pigs walked home with shoulders bent.
No gifts remained, no treats to share,
Just empty hooves and wintry air.
Yet when they reached their humble place,
Their mother met them with embrace.
No anger burned within her gaze,
But love that shone in golden rays.

"My dears," she said with voice so wise,
"I always knew angels wore disguise.
But never thought, in all my days,
That angels dwelled within my gaze."
And in the night, as snowflakes fell,
A tiger roared, so strong and well.
Not fierce with might, nor thirst for war,
But filled with warmth, forevermore.
For kindness sown in moments small,
Can be the greatest gift of all.

125. Who Am I If Not...

Who am I if not the giver of time,
The keeper of promises, the climber of climbs?
A silent traveller in a city's roar,
Lost in the lives that I live for.
Beneath neon lights that flicker and fade,
Among glass towers and concrete arcade,
I weave through streets of endless demand,
A shadow with burdens too heavy to stand.
The morning hums with sirens and trains,
A symphony built on ambitions and strains.
I rush through the crowd, a face in the stream,
A whisper of purpose, a fragment of dream.
Each step I take is measured, defined,
By duties imposed, by roles intertwined.
A friend, a lover, a colleague, a guide,
Yet where is the self that I keep inside?
Was I wrong to pause, to breathe, to be,
To let the world spin without pulling me?
To walk by the river with no place to go,
To watch the sunset in a quiet glow?
The office windows gleam so tall,
Reflections of those who give their all.
But in the glare, I see my face,
Fading, blurred—a ghostly trace.

The laughter I share, the love I bestow,
The patience I give when I'm weary and low—
Do they erase the longing in me,
Or build a life where I cease to be?
I gave my time, my soul, my name,
Yet still, the emptiness whispers the same.
What do I prove by being enough,
If in the end, I am lost in the rough?
I am more than the hands that serve,
More than the duty, the strength, the nerve.
I am the silence in midnight's air,
The seeker of dreams beyond despair.
So let me claim a moment alone,
A quiet retreat to a world of my own.
Let me walk where the city sleeps,
Where the lamplight flickers and sorrow weeps.
Not to abandon, not to betray,
But to gather the self I cast away.
To love the soul I failed to see,
To be, at last—to simply be.
For who am I, if not my own?
A traveller longing to return home.
A heart unchained, a breath set free—
A life that belongs to me.

126. The Poet's Heart and the Hand's Resistance

To feel is to wander through fire and rain,
To carry the stars and the weight of the pain.
The poet's heart, a beacon bright,
Sees worlds unseen, both dark and light.
It hears the wind's forgotten song,
Where time is brief and nights are long.
In every shadow, in every hue,
It glimpses something deep and true.
Yet what if hands refuse to write?
What if words dissolve in night?
The mind stirs storms yet holds them tight,
And the voice of longing shuns the light.
Oh, cruel the silence, vast the space,
When art is lost in time's embrace.
The thoughts that rise like rolling seas
Crash upon the shores of ease.
A heart so full, yet hands so still—
Is this a curse, or hidden will?
Perhaps the silence speaks in kind,
A test of soul, a trial of mind.
The poet's path is not a line,
But twisting trails where sorrows shine.

To stumble here is not to fall,
But learn to rise beyond the wall.
For art is not in perfect form,
Nor bound by rules that men have sworn.
It is the trembling, fearless leap,
The love so vast, the wound so deep.
Not every line must dance with grace,
Not every song will find its place.
But in the cracks of shattered stone,
The seeds of beauty still are sown.
To try and fail is still to dream,
To carve a path through fate's cold stream.
For even silence has its tone,
A whisper soft, yet not alone.
So, write, though words may break apart,
Let ink be rivers of the heart.
Let hands still move, though crude they seem,
For roughest hands still craft a dream.
And when the mind resists the call,
Let art take shape beyond the wall.
If words betray, then paint instead,
Let music echo where thoughts have fled.
For poetry is not confined
To careful lines of structured mind.
It dwells in dance, in sculpted clay,
In quiet steps that drift away.
And if the hand still hesitates,
If ink runs dry or canvas waits,
Then let the silence hum a tune,

Let fire glow beneath the moon.
A poet's gift is not just speech,
But how they feel, and what they reach.
To see the sorrow in a leaf,
To hear the echoing of grief.
To walk a path both sharp and wide,
To love, to break, to stand with pride.
To chase the stars, yet know too well,
That dreams are forged where shadows dwell.
So let the struggle shape your song,
Let restless nights make art belong.
The aching heart, the trembling hand,
Are threads within time's endless strand.
No perfect stroke, no flawless voice,
Can steal the rawness of your choice.
For even when the hands resist,
The poet's heart still must persist.
And though the words may twist and stray,
Their meaning finds another way.
For all creation, flawed and bright,
Is still a spark within the night.
A poet's soul is more than art—
It's how you love, it's how you start.
It's how you fight through doubt and pain,
And dare to dream once more again.
So walk this path, though rough it seems,
For even failure fuels the dreams.
To feel is art, to try is grace,
And this, dear poet, is your place.

Even in silence, you still create,
For art is born through love and fate.

127. When the Machines Took Over

The sky is dim, a hollow glow,
The sun still rises, but it feels so low.
Metal towers scrape the air,
Yet no one stops, no one stares.
The streets are filled, yet all alone,
Faces masked, hearts turned to stone.
Laughter echoes, cold and thin,
A hollow sound, devoid of kin.
Gold and silver weigh their hands,
Yet kindness slips like grains of sand.
They chase the wind, they race the tide,
Yet empty souls walk side by side.
The air hums with a restless sound,
A lifeless tune that knows no bound.
Music once a gentle art,
Now rips and tears the human heart.
Machines now breathe, machines now dream,
Of endless circuits, cold and clean.
They whisper words, they speak like men,
Yet warmth is lost, not found again.
The stars still shine, but who looks up?
Lost in screens and metal cups.

The night still falls, the dawn still breaks,
But where's the line? What path remains?
Wars are waged behind closed doors,
No swords are drawn, yet blood still pours.
A battlefield, unseen, unheard,
Where silence slays with poisoned words.
Men remain, but men are gone,
Their hearts beat on, but all feels wrong.
Their eyes once burned with hopes so bright,
Now flicker low, devoid of light.
Once the trees would sing with breeze,
Now forests weep, brought to their knees.
The rivers cry in rust and ash,
Their gentle songs reduced to trash.
The ground once warm, the earth once free,
Now grieves beneath dead industry.
Its voice is lost, no one hears,
Drowned beneath the grinding gears.
Where is love? Where is grace?
Lost within this death-bound race.
Coins are counted, numbers rise,
But hearts are lost, and truth belies.
The birds still fly, but songs decay,
Their melodies are stripped away.
The wind still calls, the ocean sways,
But who will listen in these days?
Every morning brings new light,
But who can tell the day from night?
A sunless dawn, a moonless eve,

A world so vast, yet none believe.
I ask again, I search, I seek,
Is this the life we meant to keep?
Or are we ghosts of something lost,
Drifting in this frozen frost?
Would we return if we had known,
That hearts of steel still feel alone?
That wealth is dust, that fame will fade,
And love is all that should be made?
Yet here we stand, machines in tow,
Shadows of the souls we know.
The world still turns, the days persist,
But do we live, or just exist?

Final Reflection

As the last words settle on these pages, I find myself reflecting on the journey that brought them to life. **Do We Live, or Just Exist?** is not just a collection of poetry—it is a question that lingers in the quiet spaces of our hearts, urging us to look beyond the surface of our days.

Life is often a race, a ceaseless pursuit of dreams that seem just out of reach. We run forward, eyes fixed on distant horizons, forgetting to pause and take in the world that unfolds around us. But what is the meaning of reaching the summit if we never stop to admire the sky? What is the purpose of dreaming if we never awaken to the beauty that already surrounds us?

Through these poems, I have sought to capture the essence of **living, not merely existing**—the simple joy of watching the wind dance through golden fields, the quiet wisdom whispered by the stars, the unspoken stories carried by the waves. In our search for meaning, we often overlook the greatest truth: **that life itself is art, and we are both the artists and the masterpiece.**

And then, there is imagination—that wondrous force that allows us to shape worlds beyond our own. A place where harmony is not just a distant dream but a reality we create. Within these pages, I have painted such a world—a world where nature and humanity walk hand in hand, where every soul finds its place, and where kindness is not rare but abundant.

As you close this book, I hope these verses linger in your thoughts like the last light of sunset. I hope they remind you to stop, to breathe, to admire, and to dream. Most of all, I hope they inspire you to **not just exist, but to live—to truly live.**

For in the end, life is not measured by how fast we run, but by the moments that take our breath away.

So ask yourself, as I have asked myself—Do we live, or do we just exist?

With gratitude and hope,

Titus Nazarene Kujur